HURRY
LESS
WORRY
LESS
at Christmas

JUDY CHRISTIE

HURRY LESS WORRY LESS

at Christmas

Having the Holiday Season You Long For

Abingdon Press
Nashville

HURRY LESS, WORRY LESS
at Christmas

HAVING THE HOLIDAY SEASON YOU LONG FOR

Library of Congress Cataloging-in-Publication Data

Christie, Judy Pace, 1956-
  Hurry less, worry less at Christmastime : having the holiday season you long for / Judy Pace Christie.
    p. cm.
  ISBN 978-0-687-49086-8 (pbk., : alk. paper)
  1. Christmas. 2. Holiday stress. 3. Stress management—Religious aspects—Christianity. 4. Simplicity—Religious aspects—Christianity. 5. Fasts and feasts. 6. Holidays. I. Title
BV45.C547 2007
263'.915—dc22

2007009319

ISBN 13 for Abingdon Press edition: 978-1-4267-4210-1

11 12 13 14 15 16 17 18 19 20—10 9 8 7 6 5 4 3 2 1

MANUFACTURED IN THE UNITED STATES OF AMERICA

With great love

to Melanie, Molly, Gracie, and Holli

Contents

With Gratitude ix

Introduction
Where Do You Start? xi

Chapter 1
Whatever Happened to Comfort and Joy?
Assessing Your Holidays 1

Chapter 2
Creating a New Way of Celebrating
Steps to Change Hassles to Happiness 11

Chapter 3
Developing a Thankful Heart
Using Thanksgiving to Change Your Thinking 21

Chapter 4
Glad Tidings
Savoring the Spiritual Focus of Advent and Christmas 35

Chapter 5
Less Is More
Spending Less, Eating Less, Fretting Less for More Joy 47

Chapter 6
Conquering the Clutter of Christmas
Tools to Help Move Beyond the Muddle 65

Chapter 7
The Gift of New Traditions
What to Do When Change Comes 75

Chapter 8
Special Days
Having a Happy Spirit on
Christmas Eve and Christmas Day 87

Chapter 9
Hello, New Year
Setting Goals to Start the Year with Optimism 97

Chapter 10
Growing Stronger Spiritually
Using the Days Until Epiphany 111

Resources to Help You Along the Way 123

Extras to Enjoy 131
A Sampling of Great Recipes 133
Simple Tips 144
An Advent Study for Individuals or Groups 150
A Lesson for Epiphany 156

With Gratitude

I am deeply thankful for the many people who encourage me each day as I try to be the woman God wants me to be—friends, family, people I meet at retreats and workshops, clients, colleagues, and church leaders.

I am overwhelmed by the stories and insights so many people have shared with me about Christmastime and the weeks surrounding it. Huge thanks go to the busy people who took valuable time to answer my questions on this topic and to help in myriad ways, from supporting my passion for less hurry and less worry to offering tips to help other busy people. This guidance came from special individuals like the Reverend Terri Hill, Kathie Rowell, Missy Hoagland, Karen Shideler, Pat Lingenfelter, Mary Frances Christie, Alan English, Kathy "Birdie" Turner, Kelly Butz, Jeff Pace, Diana Barber, Mary Hanisee, Mary Dark, Karen Ratzburg, Brenda McCart, Kara

Kelley, Craig Durrett, Annette Boyd, Carol Lovelady, Althea Goodwin, Mark Vasche, Monica Carter Tagore (who also has been terrific in helping me spread the "hurry less" message), and Alisa Stingley (the best personal editor a friend could have). Each of you is awesome, and I owe you big time!

I cannot tell you how much I appreciate the leaders who joyfully arranged for me to connect with special groups these past months (such as Sami Bolger, the Reverend Lys Cockrell, Dr. Judith Mower, and Susie Holton); and my "advisors" not already mentioned, including Kristy Scott; Ginger Hamilton; Jim Wilson; Rita Hummingbird; my swell Cuz, Cindy Hensley; and my wise pastor at Grace Community United Methodist Church, Dr. Rob Weber. Thanks go, always, to all the Baylor FunFest Friends and the Barret Girls, all of us turning fifty as this book was under way.

These lessons were shaped in great measure by Paces and Christies, including the brothers (Jack, Steve, David, Jackie) and their families and my wonderful daughter, Suzanne, and son, John. Thank you, too, to the friends who set a place for me at their Thanksgiving tables when I was far from home over the years—Paul and Debbie Higgs, Ed and Kim Graves, and Bob Stover and Jane McCallum.

All my efforts are encouraged and supported by the love of my husband, Paul Christie.

Peace to all of you—and thank you again and again.

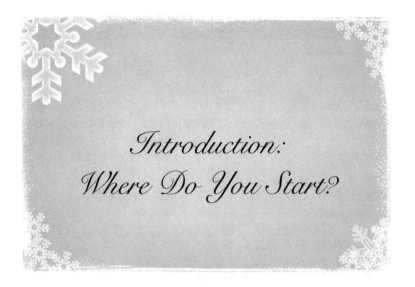

Introduction: Where Do You Start?

When I was ten or eleven years old, my mother took my little brother and me to a local store that had a large section of Christmas ornaments. She let each of us pick out one special item—an unusual treat.

Things, I suppose, were somewhat different in those days: Few, if any, stores were devoted totally to Christmas items or had huge Christmas displays that appeared early in the fall. Money was scarce, credit cards rare, and spending tight. So, the inexpensive cloth elf I chose—the one with blue hair and a striped outfit that looked like pajamas—became something I treasured. I still have that ornament, a bit pitiful now and minus one shoe that disappeared a long time ago.

That little guy reminds me of a special time with my mom, who died young, leaving me and my brothers to create new Christmas memories.

I am committed to creating such moments for special people in my life and for people God puts on my path. I fear that if I am rushing here and there, I will miss such openings—and my life will be less for it. Maybe even the world around me will be less for it. I love this time of year and want it to be a time of thankfulness and faithfulness. I yearn for a time of listening for the voice of the Father while I celebrate the coming of the Son, a time to reflect on the year just past and to anticipate the months ahead.

After the publication of my first book, *Hurry Less, Worry Less: 10 Strategies for Living the Life You Long For*, I realized that this seasonal push is almost the last straw for busy people. Somehow the distinct personalities and meaningfulness of Thanksgiving and Christmas have been molded into one big blob known generically as "The Holidays"—with a capital *T* and capital *H*. This starts way too early in November and continues until right after New Year's Day.

I watch many struggle with the challenges of the season, sometimes fed up and frazzled, wanting to pull the covers over their heads until that day when all that is left are holiday clearance tables. While leading workshops on how to slow down and enjoy life more, I found that the Thanksgiving and Christmas holidays emerged as a major challenge for most people. As I developed a new series of lessons on this topic, individuals poured out their feelings and their need to change the way they approached this time of year. These workshops were full of hope and disappointment, longing and frustration.

Many of us seek a joyful Christmas season in which we truly celebrate the birth of Christ and enjoy the people we love, and which we savor for its meaningful and fun activities. We want to jettison things that drain us and make us cranky—and we want to quit spending so much money. We do not want to feel guilty from late November until late December for not getting everything just right, for not being perfect.

Consider taking steps to accept the simple and wondrous gifts of the season, whether you are a deeply committed follower of Christ or a wanderer seeking renewal. At this time of year, we all are, deep inside, united as people who want to follow the star to the stable, who are in need of something spiritual. We can start giving true thanks for our good lives beginning at Thanksgiving and moving into Christmas and the New Year. We can adopt a more childlike attitude as we celebrate the Christ Child, appreciating the season and learning and growing from it. Our families and friends can be enriched by this approach, rather than feeling that we are hurried and worried with short tempers and long sighs.

This book offers tools to make Thanksgiving a season to build gratitude and to ease you into the busy month of December. It provides ideas about the season of Advent and about using Epiphany to grow spiritually. It gives help for remaining centered on Christ at Christmas. Perhaps you are like me and have much about the holidays that you enjoy—but some things you definitely want and need to change. You can create a Christmas that is meaningful for you and those you love, whether that means more cooking or less, more decorations or fewer. Each of us is different, and we need to shape traditions that work for us, not someone else. As the angels told the shepherds in the Gospel of Luke, "Do not be afraid." We can join together to change our approach to Christmas—and perhaps begin to bring about changes in the way the world celebrates, one person at a time.

CHAPTER ONE

Whatever Happened to Comfort and Joy?

Assessing Your Holidays

Take heart: Finding more joy in this season is possible.
Try this: Decide you will be open to ways to slow down.

> *"I bring you good news of great joy that will be for*
> *all the people. Today in the town of David a Savior*
> *has been born to you; he is Christ the Lord."*
> *—Luke 2:10-11*

In the fall, beautiful magazines and catalogues begin piling up at our house. They entice me—and they frustrate me. They show beautifully prepared holiday meals and gorgeous packages underneath elaborate trees with attractive people in elegant party clothes.

I begin to get antsy and feel as if my Thanksgiving table surely will not measure up, and my dressing will probably be dry. I start fretting that my house is not decorated adequately for Christmas. I wonder if I should trade the easy-to-cook cookies for the more elaborate ones with icing designs in multiple colors. The possibilities of the season begin to seem more like demands than opportunities.

For the past few years, I have gathered groups in early November to talk about the upcoming holiday season and to explore ways to enjoy this time of year more fully—or maybe just to enjoy it at all. These are lively, creative discussions with a rather sober thread running through them. The refrain sounds a little bit like, "Stop the holidays, I want to get off."

Discussions on this topic usually break into two sides—folks who love the holidays but are overwhelmed by them, and those who truly dread the holidays. Yes, I said "dread." On very rare occasions I run into someone who has a calm, fairly peaceful approach to the time of year from mid-November into January. This is usually a person who has simplified Christmas, choosing a minimalist approach that comes close to pretending that the holiday does not exist.

Somehow we have given up the simple pleasures and meaningful moments of this special season, trading them for more time shopping and other actions that wear us out and even tear us down. We snap at the children because we have spent too much time and money trying to find toys to make them happy. They have more stuff in their playroom and less of us. We yearn for the spiritual side of Thanksgiving and Christmas, but that seems elusive. With too much to do, we skip church, neglecting the lessons of the season for an early dash to the mall.

Little joys disappear amidst concerns of how we'll pay the credit card bills in January, how we'll juggle family gatherings and office parties and church services, how we'll get the house cleaned and decorated before company comes, and whether we need to give the next-door neighbor or the fill-in-the-blank a gift. (You know the drill: What if they give us something and we don't have anything for them?)

During holiday discussions, I am often reminded of Dr. Seuss's infamous Grinch who stole Christmas: he is a mean guy with no tenderness and lots of anger issues. Sometimes I have been known to feel that way, too, and I have encountered others who make the Grinch look like a saint. "I turn into Ebenezer Scrooge if I'm stressed," says an executive I know. Another friend told me: "I am really a whiny person, especially when I'm tired." An office neighbor says he is "the biggest humbug in my entire family" because he so dislikes "the deadening crush of Christmas commercialism."

Learning to Make Needed Changes

But it does not have to be like that. No matter how crazy the season seems to have become, we can make needed changes to enjoy the holidays and not dread them.

What happened, I wonder, to the comfort and joy we sing about in Christmas carols? Why do we, who have so much in so many areas of our lives, not feel more thankfulness?

NO MATTER HOW CRAZY THE SEASON SEEMS TO HAVE BECOME, WE CAN MAKE NEEDED CHANGES TO ENJOY THE HOLIDAYS AND NOT DREAD THEM.

Listening to other people and examining my own life, I have discovered certain themes:

1. The holidays that make up this season have lost their individuality, blending together into one long blur.

We might once have sat down to our Thanksgiving dinner with little more on our minds than how many pieces of pumpkin pie we could eat. Christmas plans would start a few days or even a couple of weeks later. Not anymore. Now, the Thanksgiving Day newspaper is filled with advertisements, begging us to plot a plan of attack for the best deals. Many Christmas decorations have been up for weeks.

This means that we enter November with a marathon in front of us—but with a sprint mentality. Before the season even gets started, it begins to seem overwhelming. This robs joy from individual occasions. Instead of a breathe-in, breathe-out rhythm that marks a measured approach to each occasion, we have a breathless feeling that says it is going to get worse before it gets better.

We need to take it a step at a time and celebrate special occasions for their specific meanings.

2. By the time Thanksgiving arrives, we realize the year is slipping by. We have been through a bit more than three hundred days and have about fifty or so left. Instead of seeing the fresh start ahead, we feel the calendar vise squeezing us.

Not only are we facing the big feed for Thanksgiving, but also we are facing a growing to-do list for Christmas. And somewhere inside we realize that all the things we were going to get done this year might not happen. The twenty pounds probably isn't going to dissolve over the next few weeks. The savings account is not going to look full and robust. Projects at work must be completed post-haste if they are to be finished this year. Time tension increases.

3. Old-fashioned though it may sound, we are swamped by the ways of the world. It is difficult to step back and assess the way we are living.

I am reminded yet again of the powerful words of Romans 12:2: "Do not conform any longer to the pattern of this world, but be transformed by the renewing of your mind. Then you will be able to test and approve what God's will is—his good, pleasing and perfect will." We are holiday conformists, despite our best intentions. We need transforming—perhaps even crave it—but we conform instead. We feel the need to buy gifts that match, dollar for dollar, those we think we will be given. We rush around trying to do it all—clean, decorate, shop, entertain, be entertained, send cards, and cook. People we have been meaning to visit all year are suddenly a necessity on the calendar.

4. Many of us put unrealistic expectations on ourselves and others during the holidays. Whatever we do, we feel it does not meet the high standards we have imposed on ourselves. Nothing is quite good enough; no amount of effort can match the glossy image we have in our mind.

As one retreat attendee said: "I've discovered a great tendency to depression during the holidays. . . . I think when we continually rev up the holiday machine, adding more and more to it, we build up our expectations for the holiday celebration to a level that we can't possibly achieve. There's an inevitable letdown when the day falls short of our hopes. I've seen this same tendency in other family members and friends." Compounding this tendency, when we feel blue we often experience shame or guilt, when perhaps we need to work through the sadness with a trusted friend, pastor, or other professional.

Instead of choosing certain priorities and focusing on them, we try to do it all. To quote one of my husband's favorite phrases: "Can't be done."

5. All of us are different. What is vital to you at this time of year may be much less important to someone else.

Some of my relatives love to get up early the Friday after Thanksgiving to stand in a dark parking lot waiting for a store to open. I want to be nowhere near a crowded parking lot on the day after Thanksgiving if at all possible. My good friend makes great fudge and homemade pecan pies for gifts. Don't ask me to do that, please. I send scads of Christmas cards with lengthy personal notes each year. Many of the people I know have given up on cards altogether.

In all of these cases, neither way is right or wrong, but clashes over such issues can open the door to tension. Compromise is required, but the more we hurry and worry, the harder it is to accommodate someone else's holiday wishes.

6. The holidays involve our families in the best ways—and the worst.

Individuals who discuss the season with me always bring up their families. Sometimes it is the in-laws or a stepparent or stepchild who is difficult or who marches to a different beat. Often it is the kaleidoscope of scheduling, trying to figure out who goes where when. For many blended families this is a special challenge, with former spouses added to the holiday equation.

Holidays with the family can also bring special joys. Some people savor time with family, planning fun events. As Karen R. says: "The day after Thanksgiving, I, along with my two sisters, Susy and Sherry, go on what we call our 'Sister Trip.'"

7. Christmas and Thanksgiving still hold many happy memories and moments for people, despite the discomfort they sometimes bring.

Most of the people I encounter want to find a better way to live and long to savor the season. Nearly all of them have something they look forward to or enjoy the most, and they want to find ways to renew their joy. My college friend Annette, a single mom and an elementary school counselor, offers a delightful sampling of this: "I like the cool weather, love the decorations and food. I like seeing people I do not always see. I like the parties, dinners, services, and celebrations. I like special times of year that cause us to reflect on different parts of our relationships with the Lord and with each other. I like the way people are more fun and festive. I like the way the season causes most people to do more for others. I like all the opportunities to minister to people during this time of year. I like hearing about what people are doing and where they are going. I like that I get to spend time with children during this time of year, because holidays are more special, fun, and exciting when you experience them at child level."

Do you see yourself in any of these themes? Are there areas that you need to tackle now?

Excavate the Possibilities of the Holidays

The possibilities of the holidays—from Thanksgiving on through Advent, Christmas, New Year's, and into the Christian celebration of Epiphany—often get buried. Perhaps this is a good time for you to consider ways to dig out those possibilities. Perhaps it is time to find ways that work for you to turn the hassles to happiness.

As Terri, a Methodist pastor in Florida, says: "I love people and being with people. I love moments that bring others joy, like decorating cookies with children or seeing someone open a big surprise present. Christmas Eve services are a nine-hour marathon that I wouldn't trade for the world. The simplicity of a little candle multiplied by the glow of all the faces is mystery and wonder. I love it."

Or as Brenda, a friend from childhood, says: "Now that my kids are adults, I put up a few things that I enjoy and go to a Christmas Eve service—very simple things. When friends ask how my holiday was, I answer, 'Quiet'—and am secretly thankful."

Nephew Jeff enjoys "the hustle and bustle of this time of year" and looks for ways to help those in need: "Give, give, and give. Help someone monetarily, physically, or spiritually. The feeling is great and habit-forming."

By starting with Thanksgiving and moving through the coming weeks intentionally, you can indeed hurry less and worry less during Christmastime. You can emerge in the New Year with a renewed spirit, ready to start fresh with a smile on your face. I propose that all of us try to live with gratitude through these holidays, awaiting the arrival of the Christ Child, anticipating Epiphany and the New Year ahead. This approach can help you set goals for your life and shape the life you long for.

My longtime co-worker Diana, a prayerful woman with a wise spirit, puts it into perspective: "Jesus came so that we can find rest, peace, and joy in him. It does not bring honor and glory to him when we wear ourselves out and become laden with chores, guilt, and debt, all for the sake of 'celebrating his birth.' I believe if we give the burden of the holidays to him, we will grow in our relationship with him."

Simple Tips from Friends

Is there a particular tradition you do not like doing? Consider not doing it.

"*I used to dread doing Christmas cards, so I quit doing them years ago.*"

"*I've already gotten rid of the tradition of getting colleagues gifts in favor of giving to local nonprofits. I participate more in office parties and bring food items for everyone to enjoy.*"

Make time to be with people you love.

"*Breaks to meet friends for lunch or dinner or just to visit really help me put things in perspective.*"

Allow yourself to get rid of unrealistic expectations and demands.

"*Make a conscious effort not to allow the retail world to dictate to you what the holidays are all about and what will make you happy. Turn the TV off, read more, listen to more music, and keep Jesus at the fore-front. He often gets uninvited to his own birthday party.*"

CHAPTER TWO

Creating a New Way of Celebrating

Steps to Change Hassles to Happiness

*Take heart: Renewed focus can help you slow down.
Try this: Imagine what your less hurried, less worried
holidays will look like.*

*God gives vision. It doesn't come from a
desire to do something good, or something worthwhile.
Vision is a gift of the Creator.*
—Rob Weber, *Visual Leadership*

My husband and I frequently go to a lake in rural north Louisiana. One of my favorite sights there is the snowy egret, a tall and slender white bird with a very skinny neck. This bird stalks slowly at the water's edge, keenly watching for a fish

FIRST WE DECIDE WHAT WE WANT OUR HOLIDAYS TO LOOK LIKE. THEN WE FIGURE OUT HOW TO MAKE THEM LOOK LIKE THAT.

for lunch. The bird's intensity is extreme, his focus unwavering. He stares and stares and stares and—zap! Lunch is served as he catches a fish and gulps it down.

The egret's attention to what he wants and the steady approach to get it is effective. So it can be with our approach to the holidays. First we decide what we want our holidays to look like. Then we figure out how to make them look like that.

Remember this: First the what, then the how.

I find that I am most likely to flounder when I do not have a clear picture of what I really want. I observe this frequently with my clients, too. It is difficult to go for what you want if you do not know what that is.

Your Joy Goal

For this extraordinary season, start by taking a few minutes to think about what you really want. Let us explore some steps that can help you select what I call your "Joy Goal." Begin to imagine—with confidence—that you can experience what you want most from the Thanksgiving and Christmas seasons. Whisper a prayer, asking God for a new vision for these days.

To get started, try using an exercise that I suggested in my book *Hurry Less, Worry Less: 10 Strategies for Living the Life You Long For.*

1. List words that you would like to describe your life from Thanksgiving into the New Year. These words become mini-goals and provide a focus for the entire season. They constitute a short, easy answer to the "what" question.

Remember our friend the egret? Following his example, keep your eye on the words you've selected and make decisions that support those words. Try to avoid being drawn off course.

If one of your words is *joyful*, you will choose activities that are fun for you and your family and avoid, where possible, those that bring you stress.

If your words are *calm* or *restful*, you may turn down an invitation or two or three. You do not have to go to every party, potluck supper, or carol sing that you are invited to. Most people understand that everyone is busy during this time of year and cannot make every event.

If you choose *debt-free*, shop accordingly. Buy smaller presents; do not pull out the plastic without great forethought.

If you choose *spiritual*, as many people do, make sure you attend the special Advent series at church and set aside time each day for personal devotions. The power of quiet time can be energizing as you head into busy days.

One friend and client chose *breathe*. Each time she found herself fretting or frenzied, she remembered that word and took a deep breath. Quickly she found herself relaxing and feeling less exhausted.

2. Make a list of words that you absolutely do not want to describe your life during the holidays. Sometimes we can figure out what we want by knowing clearly what we do not want.

Begin to consider what it would take for your days to look more like the good list and less like the bad list. Perhaps you need to give up some activities. Maybe you need to add something. These are steps, often simple, that make a big difference.

You are on your way to coming up with your Joy Goal and to changing hurried and worried holidays to something wonderful.

3. List what you like most about the holiday season. What do you absolutely love? What do you enjoy each year at Thanksgiving and Christmas?

As I mentioned earlier, most people I encounter—even if hurried and worried through the season—have holiday moments they cherish and traditions they embrace. I like having the family over for Thanksgiving dinner, the one day of the year when I *really* cook. I enjoy sitting around the table with not much more to do than talk and eat, followed by a good long nap.

Moving toward Christmas, I love getting together with old friends for lunch. I can't listen to enough Christmas music—I want it in the car, the office, and at home. The day after Thanksgiving, here come the Christmas CDs, and I am sad when the time comes to put them away. I am enriched by Advent sermons, helping prepare my heart and soul for Christ. I make an extra effort not to miss church during this season, wrapping up with a joyful worship service on Christmas Eve.

Monica, a writer and business owner, opens her senses to the holidays, loving the smells and listening for joys in each day. "Smells of fruit—apples and oranges—take me back to childhood when boxes of fruit would hearken the season. The smells evoke feelings of warm nostalgia. As I've grown older, I enjoy the benevolence and good feelings of the holidays. It seems people try to be nicer, and we look for ways to help each other more. That's nice to see, especially when that can get lost in the rush-rush, buy-buy tone that can also pervade the season. I love holiday stories of giving, miracles, reunions, and rescue."

4. As you consider what you like, go ahead and admit what you do not care for about the holidays.

Be candid with yourself. Maybe you really do not like having everyone over for Christmas brunch each year. Or perhaps you are ready to *buy* potato salad—and not tell your mother-in-law! Maybe you want to change your approach to gift giving or stay at home more in the evenings. As friend Alan says, maybe you want to stop "trudging through ritualistic behaviors at the expense of spontaneous options."

Pick and Choose

Now that you have done some thinking about what you like and don't like about the holiday season, it's time to select your Joy Goal.

You are likely a smart, creative, loving person—and you know *what* you want your holidays to be like and what you want to avoid. You do all sorts of nifty things each day, ranging from taking care of children to running businesses to helping improve life in your community.

You can use those same skills and attitudes—talents you already have—to select your Joy Goal and enjoy more meaningful holidays.

I will be the first to admit that it is tough to narrow down your choices. But by choosing a main goal, just one, you can begin to make steady progress and change your holiday habits. Then, when you get that area under control, you can add another.

(OK, if you are a goal-oriented overachiever who has to have more than one, go for it. But do not come up with so many that you lose focus and let the prize slip away. Remember the keen, steady, focused eye of the egret.)

This narrowing process is somewhat similar to going to a fantastic buffet. I am reminded of one I attended while in south Louisiana for a wedding. That meal had so many delicious items that I did not know where to start—poached eggs with crawfish on top, bread pudding, homemade omelets and waffles with all sorts of fresh berries, salads galore, fish. You name it and it seemed to be there.

Now, the problem with great buffets such as this one is that we cannot possibly eat everything. We must pick and choose, savoring special things we do not usually have and avoiding things that don't seem worth wasting stomach space (OK, and calories) on. In the most basic sense, this is how your Joy Goal works. You are only putting the best on your plate; you cannot do everything. You cannot have everything. You must make choices.

What tops your wish list for the holiday season? Perhaps you want to establish warm and loving memories for your family, or perform some sort of volunteer service for people in need. Maybe you want to spend more time in prayer. Possibly you crave a relaxed gathering with old friends, focusing on telling old stories and not on the cost of gifts. Maybe your number-one wish is to get to January without huge credit card bills. Or maybe you want to be more organized at work so that end-of-year projects do not swamp you and keep you from enjoying the richness of these days.

How to Get There

After selecting your Joy Goal (the *what*), it's time to think about achieving that goal (the *how*).

What steps do you need to take to make your Joy Goal come true? What do you need to do? What do you need to stop doing?

List about a half dozen things you need to do or stop doing to make your Joy Goal come true.

Maybe you will decide to pay attention to Thanksgiving, savoring the blessings of your life and committing to give thanks each day from the first of November into the New Year. If one of your goals is to have a more financially sensible holiday season, you might set a dollar amount for gifts or decide to spend less on each gift. You might commit to spending an hour working up a

17

holiday budget and deciding on a system to keep track. Maybe your goal is to have more relaxed time with your children—so you need to block out time on your calendar. Make that time as sacred as the time you set apart for the big Christmas gala or office party. You might want to come up with a list of fun activities for that time.

Mark, a West Coast friend and colleague, says, "Eliminate or at least minimize the thieves of joy—the things you know will create stress. Just say no to the things that stress you out and make you feel like a contestant on 'Survivor: The Holidays.' "

Maybe your goal is truly to live one of the words you came up with to describe your life—a word such as *peaceful.* Perhaps you will decide to have a certain number of nights at home each week or to attend church each week or to have an Advent study time each morning. Perhaps you want to start the New Year with written goals or commit to pray for God's guidance from Advent until Epiphany.

Perhaps you have a more practical idea, such as friend Craig's suggestions for "planning at work, building in mini-deadlines to get things accomplished."

As you write your steps, consider what brings you comfort and joy during the holidays. Build in small rituals that help you relax and renew. I like to drink my morning coffee out of a Christmas mug and listen to Christmas carols in the morning. (Did I mention that I like Christmas music?) I like to do an Advent study during my morning quiet time. I like to drive my young niece around to look at Christmas lights. Each of these rituals is small but helps me savor the season.

Simple Tips from Friends

Want to savor the holidays more?

"Make lists. Start early. Save at least one night a week to do nothing except what you find restful."

Rediscover favorite things.

"During the holidays I reread two of my favorite stories."

"It helps me to read Christmas-themed literature, whether fiction or religious nonfiction."

Keep a Christmas journal.

"I cannot say how helpful my Christmas journal is. I make sure I put down what I learned, what I want to change, ideas I have for next year."

CHAPTER THREE

Developing a Thankful Heart

Using Thanksgiving to Change Your Thinking

Take heart: Anything that can go right will go right.
Try this: Look for the good in each day.

For all that has been—Thanks! To all that shall be—Yes!
—Dag Hammarskjöld

My life has been amazingly blessed. Perhaps like you, I have plenty to eat, lots of "extras," people I love, and people who love me. The challenges of life can be dealt with, and the good days far surpass the bad ones.

But, regrettably, I have too often chosen to focus on what I do *not* have. My thoughts are prone to wander to what I *want*, what I *need*. Weird little greedy thoughts seem to occupy too much of my brain on some days, tending to make me focus on what is wrong rather than what is right, on what I do not have rather than what I do have.

Through the years, however, I have begun to realize that these thoughts can be silenced fairly easily. When that grabby thinking starts, I must stop and give thanks.

I have found that giving thanks is powerful medicine for almost anything that ails me. One of the joyful truths of our lives is that even on the gloomiest, saddest, most tense days, we have much for which to be thankful. On the *really* hard days, just the process of putting together such a list can yield amazing results.

When you are having one of those days when things seem to be going every which way but right, you can change almost anything by focusing on what you are thankful for and not dwelling on what is not working. That is why the Thanksgiving season can be such a powerful time to start living the life you long for—or to get back on track if you have lost your way. Changing your approach to Thanksgiving can help you add immense joy not only to your holiday season but to your life. Start with Thanksgiving week, and prepare to move through Christmas and New Year's with an entirely new and wonderful outlook.

A Sweet and Special Time of Year

Most of the people I know are nearly obsessed with time—not enough time, how fast time is passing, where the time goes. Part of the way we live is by annual markers, those events that roll around year in and year out, reminding us of the passage of time.

For many people, Thanksgiving marks the beginning of "The Holidays," that time of year when you feel as if you have more to do than you will ever get done. But what if you slowly began to change this outlook? What if, instead of the beginning of the hectic, harried, sometimes hurtful holidays, Thanksgiving heralded the beginning of a sweet and special time of year? What if it became a season when you began anew to focus on what really matters to you and what you want from life?

How might that work? And, if it did, how might you feel?

Thanksgiving does not have to be the launching point for weeks of too much—too much food, too much spending, and too many activities. It can be the starting point of a new way of living and thinking.

This is not as hard as it may sound.

First, in early to mid-November, take a few minutes to begin thinking about what you want your holidays to look and feel like. Consider how you can end the year in a strong and happy way and start the New Year with hope and joy. Most of us do not have time for long periods of solitude and reflection. But we can find moments here and there to assess how we *are* living and how we *want* to live. No matter how busy we are, we can find time to do the things that matter the most to us.

When you start thinking about who will carve the turkey, carve out some time to think about the season. Grab a notebook or tablet and begin to jot down your heart's desire for this time of year and a step or two that you can take to create a more joyful season. (In later chapters, we will discuss more ways to do this, but for now, agree to step back and begin to reflect on Thanksgiving as a gate to something amazing.)

Now list what you are thankful for. List twenty things. Then list twenty more. Keep at this until you have at least one hundred items written down. You will start with the most obvious: perhaps your spouse and children, good health, a special friend. But as you list more, you will begin to think about smaller things you enjoy and are thankful for: a moment in a comfortable chair drinking coffee in the morning, or a visit with a neighbor on the porch.

Continue.

Go deeper.

As you do, you will begin to notice your surroundings with a new appreciation. You may realize that you really love that huge pine tree in the front yard or the way the sun rises over the house across the street or that big hug you got from your granddaughter as she was preparing to go home.

More Thanks, Less Worry

As you begin to give thanks more, you will find that you will worry less. It is as though gratitude begins to take up the space in your mind and heart where worry used to live. God draws near to us when we give thanks. We are aware of the divine Presence in our lives, guiding us, listening, providing.

The Bible puts it this way: "Be joyful always; pray continually; give thanks in all circumstances, for this is God's will for you in Christ Jesus" (1 Thessalonians 5:16-18).

For many years I have been intrigued and inspired by what the Bible says about giving thanks. The direction is quite straightfor-ward: **We are to give thanks in everything, for everything.**

Give thanks for everything? But

GOD DRAWS NEAR TO US WHEN WE GIVE THANKS. WE ARE AWARE OF THE DIVINE PRESENCE IN OUR LIVES, GUIDING US, LISTENING, PROVIDING.

what about the problem I am having in my family or the money troubles I am dealing with or the lousy way they are treating me at work or . . .

When you begin to think of all the things that are going wrong instead of what is going right, take a few moments with a life-changing passage from Philippians 4:4-7: "Rejoice in the Lord always. I will say it again: Rejoice! Let your gentleness be evident to all. The Lord is near. Do not be anxious about anything, but in everything, by prayer and petition, with thanksgiving, present your requests to God. And the peace of God, which transcends all understanding, will guard your hearts and your minds in Christ Jesus."

We are to rejoice in the Lord. We are not to worry. When we pray and ask for God's help, we are to do it with thanksgiving. And, of course, in the wonderful way of the Creator, when we do give thanks, we receive even more. We are given a peace that goes beyond what we could possibly understand.

As our heart fills with gratitude, we begin to notice more joyful moments. You know that feeling—when your heart swells with thankfulness, when you are touched all the way to your toes. One of these moments in my own life actually came on a Thanksgiving morning a few years ago. I got up early to go for a short jog before the day's festivities got underway. The sun was rising over a nearby park. One of the first frosts of the year glistened on the grass. It was chilly, but I knew my warm home was nearby. I thought of my new granddaughter asleep there and my children home for a few days. I thought my heart might explode, it was so full.

Most of us have moments like this when we recall the words of the Twenty-third Psalm: "My cup overflows" (verse 5b). This verse speaks of that awareness of God's special care for us and is followed by the idea that "goodness and love" will follow "all the days of my life."

Stop for a moment during the holidays to absorb what is around you and to be thankful for what is happening at that moment—whether it is the bare trees that look like a work of art with their starkness or a group of family members chatting or the taste of a dish you love.

Set aside a day of thanksgiving each week, starting in November and continuing through Advent until the Christian observance of Epiphany. On that day, focus your thoughts and prayers and words and actions on saying thank you to God. Thank the Creator for *everything* that day. When you find

yourself becoming impatient or aggravated, thank God for that moment. Your attitude will change.

When you are in one of those bad moods that sometimes swamp us, find *something* to give thanks for. "Thank you, Lord, that I am alive." "Thank you that I have opportunities to grow on these bad days." "Thank you for these shoes I am wearing. I really like the color." Always we can find a reason to be thankful, even if at that moment it is something very small.

This practice, as corny as it may sound, will transform you. (And recall the words of Romans 12:2: "Do not conform any longer to the pattern of this world, but be *transformed*."—italics added)

Unlock Joy

This transformation can be especially startling during the busy holidays. Instead of grumbling because that day-before-Thanksgiving grocery store line is so long, say thanks for food and the ease by which we obtain it. When the children drop chocolate pie on the tablecloth, be happy that they are in your life. This approach can work dozens of times in any given day and will begin to unlock a joy inside that will make you smile.

The power of a thankful heart is truly amazing. You are now celebrating Thanksgiving Day many times a year! But what about the "real" Thanksgiving Day, the one that has become so synonymous with food that we have begun to call it Turkey Day?

Decide ahead of time to use this day as it was intended—as a time to give thanks for the abundance of our lives. This may be hard when you have to cook, clean, prepare for houseguests, maybe even spend the day with some people you are not crazy about. It can also be tough when you are alone or experiencing hard times.

Think about giving thanks on this one day of the year, no matter what your circumstances. Resolve not to let the small hassles of the day outweigh the good things. Try to focus on the best about those around you rather than picking at their flaws. (After all, do you want them to obsess on *your* flaws?)

Make up your mind that you will not fret. You will not worry that the congealed salad is not congealed enough or that the corn casserole resembles a vegetable brick or that Aunt Mary wound up next to Cousin Gwen and everyone knows they have never gotten along. Tone down what one seminar participant bemoaned as the feeling of "responsibility for preparing and hosting the extended family meal."

And do not overlook the power of an afternoon nap, as my friend Mary D. says. "I have never understood those folks who insist that the meal on Thanksgiving and Christmas be served in the late afternoon or early evening. What are they thinking? That leaves no time for an afternoon nap, or what I call 'a soul purifier.' Obviously, they have never been exposed to this perfectly acceptable form of total relaxation."

Thoroughly Enjoy the Big Meal

I am what most people would call "not much of a cook." Perhaps through the years people who love to cook have spoiled me. I love to eat. But I have been a bit remiss in developing culinary skills. However, now that I am a grownup (middle-aged, some would say), I thoroughly enjoy preparing Thanksgiving dinner for my family. It seems like a small way to give back each year for the many meals they have fed me. I like the traditions of the day: the cranberry sauce that I take from the can with the rings impressed upon it, the green bean casserole that our daughter and sister-in-law like so much—yes, I mean the one with the canned onion rings and mushroom soup.

I also appreciate the items that others bring as part of our tradition—"green stuff" that sister-in-law Cid makes with whipped cream and marshmallows and some sort of pudding mix, and the gargantuan pan of cheese potatoes that sister-in-law Jane makes.

Allowing others to help with special occasion meals like this is a good thing. One person does not have to do all the work and bear all the expense. Everyone can be part of the compliments as plates are loaded down with seconds. Plus, family traditions grow and change through this process. An example: The canned cranberry sauce, which my mother served, has been supplemented now with homemade cranberry sauce that sister-in-law Isabelle makes. These two forms of cranberry sauce, sitting side by side on the kitchen-bar-turned-buffet, represent to me the past and the present. I wonder what will be added in the future?

Years ago, when my now-grown nieces and nephews were little, we started the tradition of reading Psalm 100 before the meal. Everyone gathers 'round, and we listen to these ancient words, read by one of the younger children:

Shout for joy to the LORD, all the earth.
Worship the LORD with gladness;
come before him with joyful songs.
Know that the LORD is God.
It is he who made us, and we are his;
we are his people, the sheep of his
pasture.

Enter his gates with thanksgiving
and his courts with praise;
give thanks to him and praise his
name. For the LORD is good and his love
endures forever;
his faithfulness continues through
all generations.

Even as I type those words I am struck again with how we are created to give praise, instructed to do so. Yet, I do not do it as often
and as well as I should. Thanksgiving is a precious week to begin
a new approach.

As friend Mary H. says: "On Thanksgiving, we always ask
everyone at the table to tell what they are most thankful for. Some
answers are funny, some are serious, and some make you cry." (I
have always wanted to do this, but have not convinced my clan
yet that it is worth holding up the meal for!) For pal Alisa, her
favorite holiday tradition has been quite simple through the years:
"Hearing my father say grace at the family dinner." This memory
is especially precious since the death of her dad.

Different Ways to Have a Thankful Day

Perhaps you cannot be with those you love for this special day.
Consider celebrating in a different way:

Volunteer at a local shelter that serves people in need. As you serve, you will likely find countless moments when you realize that you have so much when so many have so little. Your heart will be touched, and you will make a difference in someone's life. What feast could be better than that?

Accept the invitation of a co-worker or neighbor and eat with them. They don't know you'll be alone? Tell them. Most people do not mind having one more person to feed on Thanksgiving Day.

My family is very close-knit, so it has been especially difficult over the past twenty years when I have found myself far away and lonely for the holiday. In each case, co-workers who became good friends rescued me and created great holiday memories. The first of these experiences was in 1989, when I was a single transplant from the Deep South to the Midwest, just settling into a new job in a small town in Indiana. A friend came to visit, and she and I were at loose ends as the day approached. A co-worker and his wife graciously and generously invited us to their farm, which was overflowing with their kinfolks from far and near. We had a great time—and were introduced to stuffing made with white bread instead of cornbread. A similar experience occurred when I relocated to Jackson, Tennessee. The circulation director at the newspaper where I worked invited me over, and he and his wife made me feel welcome. The warm feeling I have for them will last forever.

And, finally, I go back in my mind to a Thanksgiving Day in Florida. My husband and I were moving, and I arrived before he did to start my new job. A co-worker at the newspaper invited me over for a memorable meal. Little did I know that my hosts would turn out to be gourmet cooks and would become our very dear friends, or that through the years I would share many delicious meals and good conversation around that table.

For those who will be with family or friends, look around for those who might be alone and invite them to share your meal and your family. Two colleagues in newsrooms in different states came up with an especially thoughtful way of doing this. They would bring a lovely Thanksgiving meal with all the trimmings to the newspaper for people who had to work that day. (The former managing editor of a Florida newspaper where I worked would even bring a linen tablecloth and candles; she has style!)

"Very Freedom"

Thanksgiving Day may be the perfect day, too, to pause and think about all you take for granted in your life. In the scurry of daily life, we often overlook major things we have to be grateful for—great things that happened or terrible things that did not happen.

In 1990, I had an encounter in Jackson, Tennessee, that reminded me of this. I flew into the small airport there from a business trip and was waiting for my luggage when I noticed an older Chinese woman who seemed distraught. Approaching her, I discovered that she had inadvertently taken the plane to Jackson, Tennessee, when she was supposed to be in Jackson, Mississippi. No more planes were leaving that day; the bus station was closed for the night. There were three people in the tiny terminal: me, the woman, and a young airline clerk. None of us knew what to do. Finally, arrangements were made for her to fly out the next morning, and I took her home with me for the night.

The woman spoke little English, and I spoke no Chinese. But somehow we managed to visit, and I learned much about her life. She had moved to the Boston area from China and had worked hard to earn a living and build a life. The road had been difficult and not without danger. I asked her why she had done it, and I will always remember her answer: "Very freedom." That encounter made me look deep within myself at all I take for granted—such as great freedom.

Begin to give thanks. It will not only change your holidays; it will change your life. Make Thanksgiving more than a day when you eat too much, work too hard in the kitchen, and thankfully usher the last relatives down the driveway. Instead, use it each year as the beginning of a season when you rejoice and marvel at the blessings in your life. This can be the starting point for learning to live with passion, enjoying each day more. And because it does roll around each year, it can be an annual reminder to stop and assess and give thanks.

By learning to do this in November each year, we can move into December and January with a renewed heart and soul.

Simple Tips from Friends

Decorate a Thanksgiving Tree, a fun activity after the big lunch.

"While the guys watched the game on TV, the ladies and children collected pinecones. We rolled them in peanut butter and birdseed. Some would string popcorn, others cranberries.

"When we were through, we would find a small tree outside near a window and decorate the tree with these homemade bird feeders. Within minutes of when we returned to the house, the birds had already started munching."

Try an active tradition or add an activity for the children.

"My favorite Thanksgiving tradition is the family football game, two-hand touch in the backyard. We have done it every year for about thirty years, so we have pictures going way back. Even though I am getting too old to play with the twenty-year-olds, I hang in there. Lots of laughs!"

"The kids usually do a play or craft to share with everyone, and we enjoy a wonderful meal and laugh about memories from years past."

Remember those who have passed away.

"Use or reuse something that belonged to a special person who has passed away. It's a perfect way to remember and honor them in a very positive manner. If you use a recipe, give out copies for future generations to keep, with your handwritten notes describing how this reminded you of someone or retelling a favorite story."

CHAPTER FOUR

Glad
Tidings

*Savoring the Spiritual Focus of
Advent and Christmas*

*Take heart: You can look forward to celebrating
the birth of Jesus.*

*Try this: Hold onto Christ during the season with a prayer for his
presence in each day.*

*Come, thou long-expected Jesus, born to set
thy people free; from our fears and sins release us,
let us find our rest in thee.*
—Charles Wesley

My niece had a baby not long ago, the first grandchild on
that side of the family, the beginning of a new generation.

Excitement permeated the preparations that went into little Holli's birth. Grandmas-to-be painted her room and neatly arranged the supplies that awaited her arrival. Friends and family gathered for numerous showers to ooh and ahh over tiny little outfits. Dad-to-be called my office with excitement in his voice when he learned he was going to be a father, and then he had to go out and buy the smallest possible Louisiana State University T-shirts and various other purple-and-gold items.

When Holli decided to arrive a couple of weeks early, phone lines were in constant use as family members passed the word. Within hours, a large crowd of boisterous parents and grandparents, aunts, uncles, cousins, friends, and co-workers had gathered at the hospital, eager, waiting. Empty pizza boxes sat nearby; bags of chips were piled in a corner. Cell phones and cameras were at the ready. Within minutes of her birth, we took turns filing into her room to marvel at the wonder of this new member of our family, adorable and tiny. We began to call others to spread the word. She was precious, and we were thrilled and thankful.

You have no doubt been part of a similar celebration—the anticipation of a long-awaited child and the exuberance and awe when the baby arrived. Perhaps you remember with a smile the birth of your own children or grandchildren, the anticipation, the amazement.

If you think about it, the scene was not all that different those many centuries ago when Jesus Christ was born. When Mary found out she was going to have a child, she went to see her cousin Elizabeth and discuss the news. Elizabeth knew this was to be a special birth and told Mary: "Blessed are you among women,

and blessed is the child you will bear" (Luke 1:42). We anticipate that special birth during the Christian season of Advent,
and we celebrate it at Christmas.

The Forgotten Season

Advent is an essential part of the Christian year, a part that
sometimes gets lost when we combine distinct seasons into one
big holiday blur. Advent has its own meaning, separate from
Christmas. As pastor Rob Weber writes in *Where Heaven Touches
Earth,* an Advent study, this "is a season of rich, rhythmic preparation for our experience of the touch of God in the world today."
He continues: "Our lives run at full speed so much of the time,
we find ourselves living somewhere other than in the moment
God has given us."

As the beginning of the church calendar, Advent helps us
commemorate the spiritual significance of this time of year and
to be part of the ancient cycle of birth, death, and resurrection.
Advent also has become a time for looking ahead to the celebration of Christmas, in churches and homes. Beginning on the
fourth Sunday before Christmas and ending on Christmas Eve,
Advent is celebrated at many churches through the use of an
Advent wreath, with a symbolic candle for each week and a candle symbolizing Christ.

Advent is important as a time of prayer and preparation for the
presence of God, when we pause and reflect on Christ and on
God's love and deliverance. By remembering that Advent is a
season in and of itself, we can begin to focus on it and on ways to

grow spiritually and sense God's nudge in our lives. Advent is also a good season to observe at home with children—through making an Advent wreath, using an Advent calendar to teach about the birth of Christ, and hanging symbolic decorations on the tree or elsewhere in the house.

Anticipating Jesus

In the weeks leading up to Christmas, perhaps you have found yourself, as I have, exhausted and impatient, worn out and wondering how many stores you could visit on one lunch hour, making to-do lists on the church bulletin during worship, wondering how you could possibly get everything done. There did not seem to be enough of you to go around!

By focusing on Jesus and beginning to anticipate his birth—the same way a family looks forward to a newborn—we can change ourselves and begin to change the world, one person at a time. Imagine that through our small, individual, heartfelt efforts we might show our families and friends and co-workers and church members a new and better approach to Christmas.

If this is what we want, how do we make it happen? Just as all eyes in that hospital room were on my great-niece when she was born, all eyes at Christmas need to be on Christ, the child and Savior.

As you take a look at your life, what part is Jesus playing in it?

First, as always when we want to consider changing, we must pause and assess where we are. We can try to do this each year in

November, our annual soul-searching to take stock of where we are and where we are going in the weeks ahead. Then we can do it again and again in the weeks leading up to Christmas. As with any habit, it will take some focus. It will not just happen.

Start by sitting quietly.

BY FOCUSING ON JESUS AND BEGINNING TO ANTICIPATE HIS BIRTH—WE CAN CHANGE OURSELVES AND BEGIN TO CHANGE THE WORLD, ONE PERSON AT A TIME.

Wow! Does that go against the grain?

Before you get caught up in the whirl of the Christmas season, plan for at least fifteen minutes alone in a quiet spot each day. If you can find more time, savor it.

Now, realistically, you will probably feel at first that you cannot do this, but finagle a few minutes to start. You may have to get up earlier a morning or two, but the peace and hopefulness this time can bring will make a mid-afternoon yawn or two worth it.

We must plan ways to sit quietly and listen for God's voice— and turn off the television, radio, and cell phone.

"Be still, and know that I am God," we are told in Psalm 46:10.

Picture this: You get up in the darkness that comes before dawn. You snuggle in a favorite chair under an afghan with a cup of coffee or tea. The house is quiet. Or, when everyone goes to bed one night, you linger, tired but hungry for a new approach to connecting with God.

Maybe you have a regular routine of praying and reading your Bible each day. Or, like many of us, maybe you struggle to find that time. Perhaps you really have not thought much of God for years but you seek something in your life and wonder if this could be it.

"Be still."

This quiet time wraps itself around you, and you open your heart to Christ. One of the many names given to the Christ Child was Immanuel, God with us. Consider in this stillness that God is with you.

"And know that I am God."

Be aware of the power and love and mercy of God.

Now, imagine how you want your Christmas season to look and feel. What if you *could* have more of these moments and fewer of the stressful and frenzied ones? What if your heart could deepen in its love for God and others through this season? What if you could reach the New Year with a new spirit? Sometimes it is easy to talk with God, and you may find this to be one of those moments. At other times, it is difficult. I find myself feeling unworthy to approach the Creator with my flaws and foibles.

Take this opportunity to offer a simple prayer to God. Nothing elaborate or poetic is required. This may be where you say, "Savior, I need your help." "God, show me a better way to live." Or, maybe it's simply: "Help!"

God tells us again and again in the Bible that prayer is heard and answered. Your words, uttered in fatigue and maybe even desperation, will be heard and answered during the season of Immanuel, God with us.

God *is* with us.

By taking even a few minutes to pray, we can begin to change how we approach the season. Then, as the busy days unfold, try to plan a few minutes each day to recall why you are doing what you are doing. Maybe you are a morning person (I am!) and can take time each morning to pray and reflect. Or maybe you are a night owl (my husband!) and prefer to end your day with thoughts of how this day went and hopes for tomorrow. Taking time each day to reflect on God's love and power is a small step that can yield big returns in how you want Christmas—and all of your life—to unfold.

As the season gets underway, I love getting up early, plugging in the tree lights, and putting on some quiet Christmas music. I write in my journal, sometimes jotting a prayer or copying a verse of Scripture that I want to think about. If I am super busy, over-tired, or feeling that I'm losing my way, I write a prayer about that, asking God to help me. I list all the dirty details of trying to do too much, losing sight of Jesus in the midst of his season, hurrying too much, and worrying too much. I ask for guidance.

Use a Journal to Reflect and Meditate

Writing in a journal can be a useful tool for this time of year. It might include a prayer, as I have just mentioned, or a word or two that you want to focus on. It might even include a busy day's to-do list, those wayward items that keep popping into your mind while you are trying to focus on Christ. Go ahead and list them and ask for God's help in dealing with them. Commit to including Jesus—with his help—in the day.

Here are some other ways to commit to the spiritual side of the holiday:

Choose a book for your own personal Advent study. My prayer is that this book might help serve that purpose for some. During this special season of preparing our hearts for the birth of Christ, I find that if I commit myself to a special study, my faith comes alive in new ways.

Attend church throughout Advent, going with an open heart to be used by God during this season. As mentioned, Advent begins four Sundays before Christmas and continues until Christmas. It marks the season leading to Christ's birth, expectantly watching for our Lord. Maybe you go to church regularly through the year but do not make it each weekend. Or you may be what one friend calls herself, a "Creaster," and only go at Christmas and Easter. Possibly you have not set foot in a church in quite some time, but the notion of Christmas has stirred something within you. You might be a devoted church attendee whose attention needs simply to be drawn more clearly to Christ.

What I find so renewing about Advent is the way it helps me turn off the crazy commercial side of my brain and re-focus on Christ as the holidays get busier. Many churches have a series of sermons intended to help prepare hearts and minds for this holy celebration. Some churches have evening Advent groups that meet for meditation and discussion. Others have morning prayer time.

Serve other people. When we get so caught up in "I, me, mine" during the weeks leading up to Christmas, we too often overlook opportunities to serve. Making time for these opportunities can enrich our enjoyment and understanding of this time of year. Most of us have so much, but our communities are filled with people who have little. These are people who have fallen on financial hard times or who have health problems or who are alone or who hurt for one of a hundred reasons.

Volunteer in some way as part of the way you and your family celebrate Christmas. It is amazingly powerful to pray that on my path God will place people who need help. I am somewhat ashamed to say that I also must pray that when those people do come along, I need to be alert to and aware of them, willing to help, and not blinded by my own selfishness and judgmental nature.

Include manger scenes in your decorations. These are a simple reminder of why we are celebrating. A young dad told me that putting a manger scene in every room "reminds you of much."

Reread the Christmas story in the second chapter of Luke and rethink its meaning. Sometimes the most familiar stories become routine to us, and we forget to listen to the words. I regularly find that God guides me through well-known stories in fresh ways, when a certain word or verse draws my attention. As we grow and change, old stories can have new meanings. Read the awesome story in Luke 2 with a prayer that God will speak to you through it in new ways.

One approach that helps me explore a Bible story is to consider how I might have reacted had I lived in biblical times. For many years I was a journalist, and I think about how I would have felt had I been observing Bible events firsthand. Or sometimes I think about what I would have done if I had been a character in the story. Often I feel a bit sheepish, suspecting that I would have been one of the complainers, the fearful, the uncertain. But then I try to imagine how Christ would have responded to me. I take heart in his love and forgiveness.

You may be thinking that you are just not up to any of these approaches. You may feel overwhelmed and under pressure. You may be searching but not sure where to start, wandering through this spiritual season with a wallet full of plastic and a heart full of dismay. Remember these words (mentioned several times in the Bible): "Be strong and courageous. Do not be afraid or discouraged" (1 Chronicles 22:13).

Consider praying this Christmas prayer:

"Come, Lord Jesus. Come into my heart, into my life, into these busy days. Be part of my thoughts, my words, my actions during this season in which we celebrate your birth. Amen."

Simple Tips from Friends

Take time to go to church during this season, even when you feel too busy.

"I love the way we celebrate the birth of the baby Jesus at church—the special services and music."

"Go to church. Not as an afterthought but truly searching for Christ. I need to be reminded of the reason for the season every year. I make myself remember, 'Seek ye first the Kingdom of God and all other things will be added.' It works!"

Make time for uncomplicated joys.

"Listen to music, lots of it, with all the lights out except the Christmas tree lights. Play with children. Look for the ways God surprises with meaning. I believe the first Christmas was a major surprise in many ways and that God still comes in unexpected ways, especially when we look for them."

Recognize that the pressure to conform to society often robs us of the beauty of the season.

People should try to "be pleasers of God and not people pleasers (best gift, best meal—best, best, best)."

CHAPTER FIVE

Less Is More

Spending Less, Eating Less, Fretting Less for More Joy

Take heart: You do not have to buy expensive gifts.
Try this: Do not overspend.

But I know something else looms out there, something stronger to
those who discover it: the life of the Spirit frees people from the
compulsion of grasping and accumulating, and makes it possible to
ride the slow flow of time and finally see the waiting world.
—Ray Waddle, Against the Grain

One of my favorite Christmas memories occurred about thirty years ago when my first two nephews were toddlers. You probably have a similar memory.

As we gathered for our annual Christmas Eve family party, each aunt and uncle was proud of the gifts chosen for these cute new members of our family. And perhaps each of us secretly hoped that our gift would be the one that the children liked best—the stuffed animal that would become the beloved toy that went everywhere with the family, the book that would be dog-eared and memorized after frequent readings.

Much thought had gone into these early gifts because much was at stake—including the favorite aunt or uncle prize! As you probably already suspect, these two tots fairly quickly set the gifts aside. They began to play instead with the boxes and discarded wrapping paper, totally thrilled by the fun of this new game.

Looking now at these two grown men, it is hard to imagine them toddling over and climbing into a cardboard box, squealing. But it is easy to see that we need to simplify our approach to Christmas to find more joy. In probably no area do people pour forth more feelings about the need for change than on the topics of spending too much and eating too much and doing too much.

From Thanksgiving through Christmas and on into the New Year, remember: Less is more. Everyone has more than enough candy, perfume, knickknacks. Err on the side of less. A little scaling back can be a good thing. Spend a little less than you intended on a gift. Eat and drink a little less. If one plate of hors d'oeuvres is great, two are not necessarily better.

I can think of only two exceptions to the "less is more" rule at Christmas. One is prayer and the other is sleep.

Pray More

Decide to pray more during this season—for the people you love, for your attitude during the holidays, for your devotion to Christ, for people in need.

One friend prays for those who are alone. "I start praying prior to Christmas for God to show me any people who do not have a place to eat Christmas dinner. I want to extend the invitation early, so they know they have a place to eat. We have a small family, and it has been easy for us to add people to our table, and we have benefited from having them."

Plan to get more sleep.

During the hectic holidays, a good night's sleep is not likely to happen without a plan. Do not schedule activities for every evening and weekend moment, leaving only the hours between midnight and 6:00 AM for wrapping, baking, card writing, online shopping, cleaning, and decorating. (A former co-worker says she knows she has to allow time for at least eight hours' sleep three to four days a week during the holidays. How much sleep do you need to be a kind and loving person during this season?)

The "less" approach to the season is extremely difficult.

The world seems to focus on more, more, more, bigger, better, more intricate and elaborate. A woman who attended a retreat with me in Florida said, "I am cranky around the holidays when I eat too much, don't get enough sleep, and don't exercise. I need to take care of myself so that I can really enjoy it."

How can you focus on simpler, kinder, smaller, more sincere? Consider these steps:

Return to your thoughts of how you want your holidays to look and feel. Consider the words you chose to describe your life. Begin to pray anew that God will speak to you about how to shape your days accordingly. Ask for guidance.

Decide that you will take at least a few steps to simplify your holidays. Begin to think about what those steps could be. Perhaps one is cutting out the Christmas party you have had for the past dozen years. Or maybe you will decide to buy each of your co-workers a small ornament rather than trying to make each of them a gift or buy them something more elaborate. Maybe you will ask the family to make this year's Christmas Eve supper a potluck rather than having one person do all the work.

Figure how much money you can spend for Christmas gifts—not how much you *want* to spend but how much you actually have available to spend. In my work, I find that money is one of the key stressors in most people's lives, even if they make quite a good living. "I dread the expense, the preparation for parties, the excessive gift buying that can leave you exhausted," a former client said. "I hate knowing that I will be paying these bills for the whole first quarter of next year."

Deciding how much you will spend, how much you can afford to spend, is a key step. It is one of the first steps each of us should take in trying to make our holidays less hurried and less worried. Buying excessive gifts requires lots of time for shopping. This makes people hurried. It costs a great deal of money, often money people do not have on hand. This causes worry. In addition, the focus on buying and spending causes other sorts of worry —that you have not found the right pres- ents, that what you bought is not good enough, or that the recipient will not like it.

I HAVE COME TO REALIZE THAT WE NEED TO SPEND LESS MONEY ON PRESENTS AND MORE TIME WITH THE PEOPLE WE LOVE.

Stop.

I love presents—both giving and receiving them. I like sur- prises and receiving the gift that shows the person really knows me. (For example, some of my favorite presents through the years have been journals, chosen by friends and family members who know I fill them up at an absurdly rapid pace.) I love to find the right gift for someone—the embroidered quilt with dog designs in a thrift store for a friend who loves pets, the cute purse for a young friend.

But I have come to realize that we need to spend less money on presents and more time with the people we love, that we need to enjoy being together during the holidays and not fret that our presents will somehow come up lacking.

This is not a contest.

I do not advocate not giving gifts. I think we show people we care about them by remembering them on such occasions. But I propose having more fun with it, doing it with a happy heart instead of dread and fatigue.

Take thirty minutes of your shopping time one lunch hour or evening and do some soul-searching about gift giving and the accompanying expenditures. As you contemplate the gifts you will buy, what and for whom, consider giving to people you want to give to, not people you feel obligated to give to.

Make a list of the handful of people to whom you definitely want to give. These folks, I think, generally fall into four groups. The first three groups are closest family (spouse, children, parents, and grandparents), other family (siblings, aunts and uncles, cousins), and friends (including co-workers you might want to give a present to). The fourth group is a bit different; it is composed of people who serve you during the year (pastor, mail carrier, your favorite waitress at the neighborhood coffee shop), those you encounter who might need a little love and attention at Christmas, and people who are in great need. Sometimes these are names you pick up at church. Or, maybe it is someone you notice who has a sudden reversal of fortune during the holidays. Perhaps it is a friend who is recently divorced and lonely or an older person whose children live far away. Being open to these people can help you reclaim the delight of giving gifts at Christmas, buying for people who are deeply grateful and who have a need.

Years ago, I had a clear example of this kind of situation. I was working at a newspaper, and, in mid-December, we ran a news story on a mobile home fire in a nearby community. A mother and children had lost everything. Someone in the newsroom suggested that we take up a collection and buy gifts for this unknown family. A colleague collected the money, and she and I headed off to a local discount department store. We each grabbed a shopping cart and set out to find two gifts for each child and the mother. We were not sure exactly how much money we had to spend, but we figured if we needed to chip in some extra, that's what we would do.

When we checked out, the total was just over a hundred dollars. We pulled out the envelope with the donations in it and counted it out. We were within a couple of cents of what we had spent.

I still get chill bumps when I think of that magic Christmas moment.

Do not overlook people around you who might be in need or just need to know you were thinking of them.

Take Some Names Off Your List

Once you have come up with the people you most want to give to, consider people you have been giving to who might need to come off your list. These are people you give to out of habit or obligation. If you have been giving a gift to a neighbor you lived next door to five years ago and rarely see anymore, consider stopping that. Send a card instead. Or make a donation to a charity you like in that person's name. Slowly ease out of the "obligation" gifts.

This can be done tactfully, even though it makes us uneasy. We worry that the person will give us a gift and we will feel embarrassed. If they do give a gift, smile and say thank you. Do not make excuses or pretend that your gift for them is at home under the tree. The person may feel relieved that next year they do not need to give you a gift.

Also, consider spending slightly less on each present, boldly giving up that annual worry that your gift will look cheap compared with what someone gives you or what someone else gives them. Perhaps your family will be relieved if you suggest a slightly smaller approach to gift giving. One friend said, "I wish my family could downsize the gift giving. We seem to go overboard at Christmas." If you really want to give lots of gifts, consider spreading some out through the year when they might be appreciated more or come as a happy surprise. Children often have so many things on Christmas that many get tossed aside quickly.

Donations can make meaningful and easy gifts, allowing your money to go for something that will not collect dust or wind up in a garage sale. As Kara, a former missionary, says about this practice: "What an exciting thing to know that gifts are helping others."

Many people in my workshops admit that they obsess with finding the right gift, often spending excessive time trying to make a decision. Others say they have, out of desperation, moved beyond that: "I don't like feeling compelled to find the 'perfect' gift, so I've stopped trying. A good gift is good enough."

Different people have different resources and are at varying points in life. In our family, for example, we have young married couples just starting out with little money. We have middle-aged couples whose resources are stretched by expenses ranging from college tuition for the children to medical bills. We have retired people and people at the top of their careers who are making pretty good money.

Clearly some people have less to spend than others.

Do not try to match dollar for dollar. This ruins the spirit of giving and can turn a fun family gathering into a massive spending free-for-all.

Families handle gifts in different ways.

Some draw names, a change in tradition that we have recently made with my brothers and their families. This eases the financial burden of the holidays and cuts down on the time spent shopping. In addition, this change can turn the focus away from gifts and onto visiting. Many families also set a spending limit on the gift, so that family members are less likely to feel pressured to spend more than they can afford.

The truth is that few of us need much, and we often have extra items lying around the house. While gifts can be nice, they also can add to the clutter of our already full homes.

A college friend's family buys everyone a gift that costs no more than five dollars—a mug or a fishing lure or other small item. Other families give gifts only to the children when the extended family gathers. One retreat participant said her children receive only three gifts from their parents, using the gifts of the Magi to Christ as their guide. "If three gifts were good enough for baby Jesus, they are good enough for my children," she said with a smile. In addition, Santa brings one gift and Rudolph brings a gift. The latter is generally something for outdoor enjoyment, sometimes for the whole family. In one friend's family, the siblings make gifts for each other's families each year. They use their talents and interests to come up with something that is not too expensive and is personal.

We often feel pushed into the excesses of the holidays. This reminds me of how I feel when people zoom up behind me on the interstate. Even when I am driving a bit faster than I probably should, I feel that I should go even faster.

The Christmas rush is sort of like this in my life. I know the speed at which I want to live, but I too often let people begin to push me into spending more or doing more than I want or need to do. This is my problem, though, and not that of the people riding my bumper.

We can decide to go at a slower speed. We can make changes. **The amazing thing is that even small changes can make big differences.**

One, we feel better and not quite so out of control.

Two, others begin to feel a sense of relief, and we have a positive influence on them.

Three, we can have a positive impact that expands beyond our home or office as people begin to try this approach that they have observed in us.

Coming Up with a Spending Plan

Once you have a pretty good idea of whom you will give gifts to, work on your holiday spending plan. This is a guide for how much money you will spend. Even though you may hate the word *budget*, a spending plan will be a tool that can help you make it through the holidays with much less worry. Set aside an hour or so to work on your holiday budget. Estimate the cost of gifts, based on the list you have made of recipients. Add the estimated expense of food at Thanksgiving and for any entertaining you do during the Christmas season. Include travel costs, if you travel to see family or friends. Other possible costs: donations to your church or favorite charities, postage and the cost of cards, any new decorations you plan to add, gift wrap supplies, and so forth.

Try to be realistic as you draw up your spending plan. When it comes to estimates, get it wrong on the high side. Then you will be pleasantly surprised rather than dismayed. As you learn to plan for less hurried and less worried holidays, it will become easier to stick to a spending plan. One way is to save a little money each month throughout the year to help pay the Christmas bills. Some banks and credit unions offer Christmas Clubs for this, with higher interest rates than regular savings accounts. Or if you are disciplined, you can do it yourself, putting money into your savings account each month. If you do this, you will have to resist pulling it out in the summer for your vacation or for that new outfit you want in the early fall.

Another approach is to buy gifts as you find them during the year, often getting the right item at a better price. A caution here is not to buy without specific people in mind. I have found that in trying to be thrifty, I wind up spending extra on impulse gift buys that really are not suited to the people on my gift list. Keep a list of what you buy, so that you do not forget and duplicate your efforts along the way.

If You Are in a Financial Bind . . .

You may find yourself in a hole already for the Christmas ahead. Perhaps you find it hard to make ends meet, and you have no money set aside. If so, the thought of trying to finance the months of November and December probably causes a knot to form in your stomach.

Take a deep breath and decide to cut back drastically.

This is possible, although it may not feel pleasant at first. It may mean that you and your spouse give each other fewer gifts or spend much less on your children, or that you decide to draw names with your siblings even though you have previously given gifts to all of them. It may mean, quite simply, that you give gifts that cost very little. Resist the urge to charge lots of gifts on credit cards that will come due in January and get the New Year off to a strained start. If you do charge, do so with the discipline that you will pay the balance immediately. Also remember that often property taxes and other annual expenses pop up at year's end, adding to the financial strain.

While most of us like receiving nice things, we usually are not concerned about the price of an item. Few people would choose a nice gift over peace of mind for the giver. If you are giving to people who seem to be ringing up a cash-register tally as they open gifts, then they have the problem, not you. If you worry that your children's pile of loot will look puny in comparison with the neighbors' gifts, remember that you are teaching your children an important lesson about the meaning of the season. In addition, most kids have so many toys already that they cannot play with them all. And your bad mood caused by the debt hanging over your head will not be worth it.

Let me say again that I do not subscribe to the "bah, humbug" theory of Christmas. But I hear so many people complaining about gift giving at Christmas that I find it of deep concern. For many people, it has turned into an expensive obligation, or an indication of how much money they have. Give those thoughts up. If this is extra hard to do, pray about it. When you start fretting, start praying. I think my friend Birdie sums it up very well: "I am a firm believer in staying within the funds in my Christmas Club. I don't think Jesus would appreciate us being lousy stewards of his precious Father's resources, in the name of celebrating his own birthday."

When we let our attention become so focused on giving and spending, the commercial Christmas wins over the meaningful Christmas.

To Overeat or Not to Overeat

While money is the number-one worry for many people during the holidays, overeating is way up there on the list. From the moment the turkey is carved on Thanksgiving Day until the black-eyed peas are eaten on January 1, we eat. And eat. And eat some more. We eat at home. We eat at the office, where food magically appears in The Usual Spot. We eat with our small group at church. We eat with old friends we only see once a year.

To add to the challenge, we are so busy that we cut back on exercise.

Surveys show that the average person gains several pounds a year during the holiday season. Those of us who have tried so hard to be good about diet and exercise during the year often go to one of two extremes. We count the calories in every bite of cheese dip and cookies and drive everyone around us nuts with our obsession. Or we throw to the wind any thoughts of weight and eat everything in sight. Neither is very effective.

The holidays are a good time to keep exercising, resume exercising, or start exercising.

Physical activity can clear the mind and help you relax. Part of the urge to hurry and worry will evaporate under the influence of a little exercise. In addition, you can eat those half dozen strawberries dipped in chocolate or that piece of pecan pie without feeling guilty. Start small. If you have not exercised in a while, you should get checked out by your doctor.

If you have been a so-so exerciser, do not start out with an hour a day, seven days a week. You may quickly hurt yourself or burn out. Instead, commit a few minutes several days a week for a walk or a run, or a visit to your gym or health club. Use the time to focus on what is right with your holidays and what changes you might want to make. Perhaps you will simply choose to go for a walk around the block—and unexpectedly discover insights you need to move ahead.

Enjoy the delicious foods of the holidays, but do not gorge. Resist the urge to eat seconds and thirds. Choose the desserts you love the most; do not eat everything in sight just because it is available. Drink plenty of water.

Activity Overload

One reason we lose our joy from Thanksgiving into the New Year is that we overdo, overplan, overschedule. By trying to do everything, we find ourselves not having much enjoyment at anything. Our calendars become so full that trying to find time for a holiday lunch visit with a friend turns into an ordeal.

Put your calendar on a diet.

Learn to say no to some events and gatherings. As I mentioned in my first *Hurry Less, Worry Less* book, when you say no to one thing, you are really saying yes to something else. So perhaps you are not going to your book club's annual party because you want to attend your Sunday school class party. Or maybe you want to stay home and watch a Christmas movie with the children rather than go to a friend's house. One couple we know allowed each of their young children to plan a Christmas event, and the family did it—"something like going out to Burger King with another family or going to look at Christmas lights."

Keeping my calendar trim during this season is very hard. I enjoy being with people. I do not want to miss anything. I certainly do not want to hurt someone's feelings by turning them down. But I have discovered that if I try to go to everything, I am worn out and impatient, and I wind up not enjoying the season to the fullest. So, I try to balance evenings out with evenings at home. I try to leave some lunch hours open, without an appointment or errand to run. I try not to juggle multiple activities on one evening. While I may feel I need to attend a function, such as something related to work, I slice and dice my schedule so that it does not become one big blob of places I "ought" to go.

I also consider my family during all this hustle and bustle. Something I might really want to attend might not be fun at all for my husband. On the other hand, he might have something he wants to do that I would just as soon avoid. We have found that compromising helps us avoid too many events where one of us is a bit uncomfortable.

In addition, I try to consolidate my shopping. For example, on a weeknight in early December the mall is often not too crowded. I take my gift list and work my way through it, steady and focused. I do not rush, but I do not dawdle. I make good progress. Feeling the need to run here and there on every lunch hour and after work each day in December wears me out. It is draining and often results in spending extra money.

Stop Trying to Be Perfect

Few things in life are perfect, but many things are wonderful. So it goes during the holidays. We do not have to be perfect. Our houses do not have to be spotless and our decorations like something out of *Pretty Home* magazine. Our dishes do not have to sparkle and our food all be homemade. It is OK to pick and choose what you will spend your time and energy and money on. It is more than OK.

By doing less, fretting less, worrying less, you can enjoy the season more. In addition, the people you are doing much of this for will find you a lot more enjoyable to be around.

So make yourself a cup of hot chocolate; put your feet up; listen to a favorite Christmas CD. And remember: Less is more.

Simple Tips from Friends

Be more budget conscious.

"I realized that most people don't remember what you get them and really don't care. It's the idea of being remembered. Try to stay within a set spending limit. I did that this past holiday, and it made the season less stressful for me because I wasn't accumulating debt."

Organize your shopping, spending less time on it.

"Shoppers remind me of bees buzzing around honey. Sometimes if you get in their way you get stung."

Give something of yourself.

One friend's husband *"every year on Christmas Eve writes each of us a letter in which he speaks to us from his heart and tells us how he feels about us and the past year. The letters are treasures. Just writing this and thinking about them makes me cry."*

CHAPTER SIX

Conquering the Clutter of Christmas

Tools to Help Move Beyond the Muddle

Take heart: You can get organized.
Try this: Simplify your decorations.

"Prepare the way for the Lord, make straight paths for him."
—Matthew 3:3

M ost people I know have a day each season when The Decorations Come Down from the Attic or Out of the Closet. This is a very scary day.

You know the feeling.

One minute the house looks reasonably OK.

The next? Complete clutter and chaos.

What is a busy, well-meaning person to do?

I am reminded of a small flower bed in our yard. It has an azalea bush, a little purple flowering tree, some irises and snapdragons—and a tenacious vine that wants to take over the entire space. No matter how much I attack that vine, it keeps slowly invading, inch by inch. After last summer's vacation, I returned to find that it had nearly choked out the entire bed.

Such is Christmas clutter.

Decorations, gift-wrapping supplies, and presents can easily encroach on the entire house, choking out the breakfast table, the coffee table, the bed in the guest room. Before you know it, you can barely stand to walk into the house, knowing what waits. Even if you love pretty packages and lovely decorations, this disarray threatens to overwhelm. Spiritual peace and joy are hidden under a big untidy pile. You can't prepare a straight path for the Lord's birth with a house and mind encumbered with stuff.

However, you can win this battle—and in so doing will open up time and energy and mind space for simplicity and renewing your spiritual focus. In the same way that I beat the greedy vine with some fierce weeding, you can tackle this morass at your house. Clearing clutter can free up time for a few minutes of meditation or reading something inspirational. Not going overboard can allow you more time to serve others who have great needs. Taking some practical steps that seem fairly ordinary can actually open up holy possibilities.

Decide how much decorating you want to do—what you and your family actually enjoy. Let go of the rest of it.

My birthday is in early December, and I have been given many great Christmas decorations through the years. Some years I like to go all out with decorations—putting Christmas items in every room. Other years I decide to take a simpler approach and only pull out a few things. I must admit that the older I get, the more I like simpler. I put out decorations I really like, and I do not feel overwhelmed by them. I know I will be much happier when the day comes that they all have to be put back in their boxes and stored for the year. (One of my college buddies says it is important to her to decorate the tree as a family. However, she notes, "Strangely everybody seems to like decorating the tree together, but when it is time to take off the decorations, nobody is available.")

Do not forget to include some decorations that are spiritual or symbolic in nature—a dove that reminds you of peace or the Holy Spirit, a manger scene that pulls you back from "all Santa Claus all the time," a candle you can light to help you focus on the presence of Christ in your life.

Decide What Works for You and Your Family

You may love lots of decorations, little Christmas villages, and a tree in every room. Go for it! Decide what you want to create and make it happen—if that adds to your joy.

One of my sisters-in-law, for example, loves Christmas and enjoys the effort required to transform her home. (Her name is Mary Frances, but during this time of year her husband renames her "Mary Christmas.") She is retired and gets enthusiastic about her holiday home. She puts a themed tree in the kitchen, sunroom, guest bathroom, and guest bedroom every year. Her "main" tree is in the living room, a big fir covered with hundreds of ornaments meticulously placed and evenly spaced. These trees are pretty, and they make our Christmas visit to her home extra festive.

She handles the messiness of all this décor and gift-wrapping by transforming her home office into Santa's workshop. She puts a note on the door: "Keep Out. This Means You!" The note is designed to keep nosy grandchildren from peeking and to keep visitors from seeing the mess behind the door. Watching her, however, it is obvious that her focus is on Christ and that her relationship with God drives the joy she gets from this season. She is active in church and shares her home and heart with others—which is important for each of us to remember as we consider why we are doing what we do.

One method to reduce clutter is ruthlessly to prune your Christmas decorations every few years. Hang onto the sentimental pieces and items you truly love. Donate the extras to a charity. Got some good things that you do not need or want anymore? Maybe your adult children want them as they get their households going.

Get rid of broken items and all those strings of lights that do not work. Face it: If you have not figured out in the past three years which of the three hundred bulbs burned out, you are probably not going to do it this year. Also, consider quickly re-reading the Christmas cards you have saved from the past ten years, pulling out a handful you really want to keep, saving the photographs enclosed, and tossing the rest of them. While I wish I had a few of the cards I have thrown out through the years, I am happy that I do not have those two trunks of mildewed letters and cards that I finally gave the old heave-ho.

Decorations present challenges both indoors and out.

I love lights; one of my holiday pleasures is seeing a string of lights randomly placed on a tree or small house, a touch of Christmas spirit here and there. I also enjoy the elaborate decorations that some people come up with, such as our across-the-street neighbors who win the neighborhood contest each year. They have a wonderful manger scene under a pine tree that reminds me of Christ's birth and a fun inflatable snowman (the kind my niece Melanie calls "puffables").

However, some people find decorating a hassle. Find what works for you, inside the house and out. Do not be afraid to take a few risks and make some changes.

One year we bought a living evergreen tree in a pot. It was scrawny but had lots of personality, and it now grows hardily in our backyard. (However, this tree did not suit the aforementioned niece, who asked her mom and dad if they could get a "fat tree.")

Try not to let your decorations—or lack thereof—keep you from inviting people over. Most folks will understand and are happy to be invited, fancy decorations or not. I recall one year when I invited some members of my newspaper staff over, early in December. My husband and I had bought a tree and put it up but somehow had not gotten it decorated, despite our best intentions. I set a box of ornaments nearby and told the guests to have at it. Several days later I noticed that one of my colleagues had put paperclips around ink pens and hung them on the tree.

One thing that seems to rob people of pleasure over the Christmas season is the notion that the house must be perfect. Most people really do not care if things are a bit messy or cluttered; they are just happy you invited them over—and relieved that you cannot see their houses.

Learn to take your housekeeping a little less seriously, not letting it be a barrier to enjoying others during the holidays.

Relax and invite a small group over for an Advent devotional, or honor a group of older people with a low-key gathering. We show the spirit of Christ in such gestures, not by focusing on unimportant appearances.

When it comes to gift wrapping, try to set aside a night or two early in the holidays to get as much done as possible. This not only makes you feel good about all you have accomplished; it clears out the storage area where you had the gifts, and it keeps you from having wrapping paper and ribbon strewn from pillar to post. If beautifully wrapped packages are important to you, go for it. If you want a faster approach, try the gift bag, which often can be done cute and quick.

Do as much as you can to make it easy on yourself. The purpose of the season is to rejoice. Lots of clutter can take away that spirit in a hurry. Do not go overboard unless this is something you truly enjoy.

Try a New Approach

One way to avoid the clutter is to use natural items, perhaps a large poinsettia plant or two, fairly inexpensive but dramatic in presentation. Another is to try something simple like a bowl of apples or a clear vase full of nuts.

Try to keep key areas free of clutter, to symbolize that the weeds of the season are not about to choke you out. I always keep the dining table clear—no papers, no newspapers, no clutter. If I do happen to wrap on the table, I immediately put the wrappings away. This is one of those habits I learned from my mother; she believed that if the rest of the house was a bit messy but the dining table was clear, things seemed better.

Try to keep up with what is coming in and make sure at least that much is going out. I try to toss most Christmas catalogues as soon as they arrive. First, they tempt me to buy things I do not need or cannot afford. Next, they take up precious time; it is easy to be lured into using my daily reading time on catalogues. Finally, they pile up faster than snow in an avalanche.

Set aside a spot for meaningful holiday mail, such as cards and Christmas letters. Put these in a basket or display them. Enjoy them. Give thanks for the friends and families they represent. Do not get so busy that you hardly give them a second glance. Our old friends the Loveladys "set them aside, then we sit down and open them together each evening after things calm down."

If you have to travel, devise a system for making sure the right gifts get where you are going. Leaving one person's gift behind is a hassle that can be avoided. Make a list of the people you are

> YOU WILL BE AMAZED AT HOW MUCH BETTER YOU WILL FEEL WITHOUT ALL THE CLUTTER—HOW MUCH MORE IN CONTROL.

delivering to. For example, each year when we head to Tennessee, we pack up two plastic containers: one for the kids and our granddaughter, one for the rest of the family. This system makes packing and transporting the gifts easier. When we get to town, it is easy to sort out presents, one more way to simplify the season.

When gifts begin coming into the house, put them away as quickly as possible. If they arrive by mail and are wrapped, put them under the tree. If the gift is something perishable, like the wonderful shipment of citrus we receive each year, put it in the kitchen.

You will be amazed at how much better you will feel without all the clutter—how much more in control. In addition, if you stay on top of this, you will avoid the need to clean up every time you have a precious few minutes to relax.

We have tried off and on over the years to clear out certain items as others came in. This is particularly useful with clothing and books and toys, items that tend to multiply and pile up. If you can put a box somewhere out of the way and fill it up before you start decorating, all the better. If not, during the season consider a ruthless approach to getting rid of extra items. These are things you rarely use or wear, and they may be of use to someone else; it is an act of stewardship and recycling.

Tidying Up after Christmas

After Christmas, different people have different approaches to putting things away. Find what works for you. Perhaps you want your tree down immediately, or maybe you want it up through the beginning of the New Year. One of my grade school friends said that her husband has a phobia about taking the tree down by December 31, because he grew up in a family that thought if they did not, they would have bad luck during the year ahead. Another friend's family always leaves decorations up until Epiphany, January 6.

Ask each person in the household to put away his or her gifts, instead of leaving them scattered around the living room. Getting things out of the way can help immensely.

When you take your tree down and begin to un-decorate the house, pull out the boxes and containers and lots of leftover tissue paper and newspapers for packing. Get things boxed up, taped, and ready for the attic or closet again. To make the process easier next year, mark on each box what is inside—good lights, best ornaments, nativity scene, and so forth. This makes it easier when you start unpacking next year, especially if you decide not to pull everything down.

Kelly, a busy mom and business owner, sums up the new approach to a less stressful Christmastime: "I think that I have released a lot of pressure to 'do it all.' If I send cards—OK. If I decorate with all our holiday stuff—OK. If not, Christmas will still be special and the coming of Jesus will still have an amazing impact on our family."

Simple Tips from Friends

Do not worry about making everything perfect.
"Instead of trying to make your house look like those in magazines, spend time with your children, grandchildren, family, and friends, doing fun things together."

Wait until shortly before Christmas to put up your tree.

"We hold off on preparations for the holidays until about two weeks before Christmas, so the entire time from Thanksgiving until December 25 is not taken up with obsessing about the holidays. We also hold off getting a tree and decorating it until the weekend before Christmas. The annual trek to choose a live tree is done with the whole family."

Allow your actions to reflect your priorities.

"Focus on the people you love and on the God who makes it all possible."

CHAPTER SEVEN

*The Gift of
New Traditions*

What to Do When Change Comes

*Take heart: Change can enrich your holidays.
Try this: Eliminate at least one tradition you no longer enjoy or that
causes you pain.*

*No wound is so trivial that the love of God is not concerned
with it. No pain is so deep, so long-standing that the
love of God cannot reach it.*
*—Flora Slosson Wuellner, from Prayer, Stress,
and Our Inner Wounds*

When I was a young girl, I was shopping at a Woolworth's store with my mother and little brother. You may remember those old stores—dime stores, they were called, and they came complete with a soda fountain and lots of little extras that caught the eye of a girl.

One of those extras was a ring-sizer, in which you slipped your finger into various sized holes until you determined what size ring you wore. Curious, I put my finger into a variety of holes until I found one that seemed to fit—sort of. But when I tried to take my finger out, it would not budge. The ring-sizer was stuck on my hand. After a moment of panic, I decided the only thing to do was to find my mom, shopping on a nearby aisle, and get her to remove it for me.

I turned to walk toward her and felt myself jerked back to the counter. The ring-sizer was chained to the counter. I was chained to the counter!

I began to try to get my brother's attention, with one of those panicky "loud" whispers you use when you are desperate but do not want to draw the attention of those around you. "Go get Mama!" I said about a half dozen times as my brother wandered over to see what I was up to. "Go get Mama!"

Before it was over, my mother, brother, a store clerk, and the store manager were trying to free me, giving me this piece of advice and that piece of advice. It was not one of my finer moments. Moistening the finger eventually did the trick, and I slid my red finger out and took my red face home.

I had not thought of that incident for years, until I started thinking about holiday traditions and why they sometimes cause us pain. Traditions, those activities we repeat year in and year out, can indeed chain us to a place we do not want or need to be. Even wonderful traditions that once fit so well sometimes become tight and uncomfortable. Some open old wounds.

Sometimes they need to be changed.

Sometimes they change whether we want them to or not.

Sometimes they need to be thrown out altogether, freeing us to try new things and new ways of looking at the season.

Our Thanksgiving and Christmas customs can be enriching and enchanting. But they also can be tedious and tiring.

As we approach the season, we can reduce hurry and worry by taking a closer look at what we do, why we do it, and whether we are in fact chained to something from which we really want to be free.

This does not mean throwing away all traditions.

Hold on to those that are still meaningful and enriching. As one friend says: "We pretty much do the same thing year after year, which I know creates stress for some people, but it works for our family and is very comforting." This friend mentions a host of traditions, including inheriting "my husband's family tradition of working a jigsaw puzzle when the family is together. It's a fun thing that pulls together all ages."

In addition, don't be afraid to try starting new traditions— activities or celebrations you try once and like, then repeat again and again.

Traditions vary widely and offer a glimpse into the lives of individuals and families. In my family, we have seen quite a few changes in recent years, as the children have gotten older and married, as some people have moved away, and as everyone's lives have unfolded.

My family's tradition at Christmas *always* revolves around Christmas Eve, the night when my siblings and our families get together. This tradition started when my parents were still alive; this was the night we opened presents and enjoyed a good meal and had fun visiting with relatives. It was one of those yearly highlights, greatly anticipated and enjoyed.

Although our parents have been dead for nearly thirty years, we have continued this tradition with much laughter and noise. We gather in the early evening at one family member's house, have a big meal, and open presents. Getting home for this was a high priority for me when I lived away. Not until I was forty-two years old did I actually miss this annual gathering—the first time in my life and the lives of my three brothers that the four of us had not been together on Christmas Eve. It has only happened three times through the years.

As you can see, this is a serious family tradition.

But we have begun to realize that we must find ways to adjust this tradition to the changes in our family. We must find ways to accommodate the new members of the group, spouses of my nieces and nephews. As I mentioned in an earlier chapter, we knew we needed a new approach to gift giving. As the family grew, so grew the pile of gifts and the cost of gifts. It had gotten to be too much.

In other ways, my husband and I have had to fashion traditions that work within my family and his and within our own home. For example, for decades the Baptist churches I attended did not have Christmas Eve services. So, getting to church and to the family party was not an issue. Then I became a United

Methodist, and the churches I attended offered the opportunity to worship on Christmas Eve. More of the children were young adults with jobs that sometimes kept them later on the holiday. All of a sudden, late afternoon gatherings were harder to juggle. We had to push them back a bit. These are small changes, really. We have been able to juggle the scheduling needs of new in-laws, and the young adults are not too far away to come home for that evening.

The Pain of Death

Many big things can affect traditions, and we need to be aware of them. One of the hardest is death. As my friend Kathie says, "Since my mother died five years ago, Christmas just hasn't been the same. But last year, we had Christmas dinner at my house for the first time, and it just felt right. I knew my mother would be proud that I had taken over her role. I hope to make Christmas dinner at my house our new family tradition."

The Christmas after my husband's mother died, we all found ourselves at loose ends on the Christie side of the family. We were hungry for a way to gather as a family, spread about from Colorado to Florida to Tennessee. We missed the annual gathering at my dear mother-in-law's house, along with that feeling of contentment from being home with family. We all knew we needed a new way to celebrate, but we were not sure what it would be.

Through the years, a terrific new tradition has evolved. We now celebrate a weekend before the holiday at the home of my husband's brother and sister-in-law, with visiting and presents and Tennessee barbecue. This tradition, though only about a decade old, has already taken on deep meaning and become part of our holiday planning.

My father died in mid-November one year. We decided that that would be the year to change our Thanksgiving tradition and eat out. I recall it as being one of the most miserable holidays of my life. We were all sad and out of our element. One of my nephews, an infant at the time, cried the entire meal. I think the rest of us felt like joining him. Sometimes you do the best you can during a holiday and hope it will be better next year. At other times, you try something new and then decide to go back to the old way.

Sometimes age and circumstances change traditions.

One colleague's family always had Christmas dinner at her mother's house. As her mother's health failed, my friend began to orchestrate the lunch, still at her mother's house. Slowly the meal moved to my friend's house. But with a demanding job and a large family, she realized that she did not feel up to having the entire group at her house each year and suggested that they rotate it.

Another way that traditions may be called upon to change is with marriage and divorce.

Since I did not marry until age thirty-five, I was used to a certain way of celebrating the holidays. My husband and I had to look for approaches that worked for us. That was fun, shaping new traditions, such as our own Christmas morning breakfast and gift exchange, eagerly checking our stockings to see what Santa might have brought.

Divorce often takes a painful toll on traditions, and new ways are often called for, especially when children are involved. This juggling of holiday visitation is extremely painful for many people and requires flexibility.

LOOK FOR NEW TRADITIONS TO REPLACE OLD FAVORITES. TRY NOT TO DWELL ON HOW IT USED TO BE, BUT FOCUS ON HOW IT CAN BE.

Look for new traditions to replace old favorites. Try not to dwell on how it used to be, but focus on how it can be. Be sensitive, above all, to the needs of the children and how to make this holiday time special for them. Pray for wisdom and discernment and forgiveness over past hurts and present pain.

Try to make holiday times special in new ways, such as the tradition of my friends who always watch a movie on Christmas Eve, or those who always have supper with friends.

If you find yourself alone or lonely at the holidays, create your own celebration. Invite friends over for a potluck supper and favorite book exchange, or volunteer at church to help with extra duties for the services that day.

If you have the good fortune to be surrounded by those you love, open your family gatherings to someone you work with who is alone in town or to a divorced friend who is struggling through a sad holiday. Share your abundance with others. Twice in recent years, my husband and I have had great fun using our airline frequent flyer miles to bring young, broke, and faraway nephews home to their parents for the holidays, once from Utah and once from New York. We got more pleasure out of those miles than we would have gotten from a trip ourselves.

A Fresh Start

When circumstances require you to change traditions, try to look on it as a liberating fresh start, a chance to try new things, to interact with other people, to offer something of yourself to someone who might need you during the holidays. The possibilities of doing something fun and creative are endless and might bring you new joys that you have not even begun to imagine.

Sometimes this is tough to do. The divorced people I know struggle mightily with the pain of being without their children on Christmas Eve or Christmas morning when the rotation is not theirs. As one woman says, even after many years there is a hole there. A client who lost her husband at a young age found she had to surround herself with friends at Christmas, making an extra effort to pull groups of people together for fellowship.

Perhaps only the touch of God will see you through a change in traditions and circumstances.

If you are at a painful place in your life, seek God's comfort. Slip into church during the holiday season and pray. Ask for the peace that passes understanding. As much as possible, recall blessings and happy times and ask God to take the sorrow.

Try to replace the magazine-picture holiday with a real one that works for you, wherever you are in your life. (And do not be afraid to ask for professional help if depression overwhelms you during this season.)

At times nothing as drastic as death or divorce affects holiday traditions. They just run their course and are not as much fun anymore. Perhaps you always loved that white-elephant gift exchange with your church friends, but now you are tired of it. Maybe you want to pull together a new group of friends for some sort of holiday gathering. Some traditions get under way but are hard to sustain. One of these for me has been a yearly post-Christmas gathering with a group of elementary school girlfriends. I love this group of women and have so much fun seeing them. But because of geography and time, we have had a tough time planning our annual lunch over the holidays.

Two old friends co-host a wonderful caroling party each year, with great food and lots of singing. However, the year that one of them was moving into a new house, the party went on hiatus. The friends took a year off, a good solution to the problem of trying to do too much.

When I was a young journalist, I would have a New Year's Eve party each year at my apartment. For a while, it was loads of fun. Then I got tired of it, in part because I'm a morning person and the very late party did not suit me, in part because it had run its course. After that tradition ended, I began having a large, informal Christmas party each year. By now I had moved into my first house, and I loved having this loud gathering where much visiting was done. Again, after several years it ran its course.

I enjoy trying things for a while and changing as needed. Otherwise, I am apt to get more caught up in the tradition than I am in the fun of the event.

Creating New Traditions

One of the ways to shape holidays that will have less hurry and less worry is to replace stale traditions with new ones that mean more to us.

Coming up with new traditions is not as hard as it may seem. First, go back to your list of how you want your holidays to look. What do you enjoy most? What do you enjoy least? Often, this will be a good guide to help you throw out, or ease out of, some old traditions and come up with some new.

As you take on new activities, you will likely need to get rid of some old ones. You cannot do everything.

Try a variety of things through the years until you find what works best for you and your family and friends. When something is OK but not great, toss it out and give something else a try. Make a list of lots of things you would do during the holidays if you had time, and begin to make your way through the list. It might take you a few years, but slowly you will begin to do more of what you enjoy and less of what drains you.

Consider what you have wanted to do for years but never have done. Decide to give one of these activities a try. It might be as small as going to an annual Christmas play at your child's school and coming home for slice-and-bake cookies and milk. Or, it might be as grand as going on a cruise at Christmas, leaving some of the confusion behind.

My list grows all the time. I want to have a brunch for my girlfriends and to cook a Christmastime lunch for the hardworking staff at my church. I want to take my niece to look at Christmas lights and have her spend the night, so her parents will have a bit of time to take care of some of their holiday errands. I want to create beautiful customized Christmas cards to send to my business clients and friends. I want to keep a great Christmas journal, writing down the happy moments and generosity of the season.

But I do not let myself fret over this list. Instead, I decide what I can do without becoming frenetic. I take stock of my top priorities—people I will spend time with, special things I will do. I get excited and hopeful about what I may try this year or next. I look at what I have added to my life and how much richer it is because of such additions, such as going to church on Christmas Eve and having lunch with a group of former work colleagues and trading favorite books.

Remember that this time of year can be joyful and exuberant. It is a wonderful time to try some new activities and perhaps to get rid of some old ones, to explore some ideas and discard others, to explore new ways to give thanks and celebrate the birth of Christ.

Simple Tips from Friends

Call upon friends for new ways to celebrate.

"Having adult children and no grandchildren slowed things down for me. I'm in several organizations, and we each plan a little get-together,

so more of my savoring the holidays is with friends over a month's time."

Whatever your traditions, focus on people.

"Simple pleasures are the best. Relationships are enjoyed most when gifts are given least and thoughts are shared about how special people have been an encouragement and blessing."

Do not take yourself too seriously.

"When we were kids we spent Christmas in the Florida Keys. It was a tradition for the kids to water-ski on Christmas morning and listen to 'Born to Run,' by Bruce Springsteen. It is a great memory, and we have miles of movie footage of us skiing, laughing, and having great fun. Just in general I need to learn to take myself a little less seriously. I think Christmas is a time when people tend to take themselves very seriously. It can be a time for depression for past life experiences or disappointment for not experiencing the perfect holiday season. I think that just simply having fun and reveling in the amazing Christmas story is a gift. A baby was born who changed the course of history. How much more simple and miraculous can it get?"

CHAPTER EIGHT

*Special
Days*

*Having a Happy Spirit on Christmas Eve
and Christmas Day*

Take heart: Cling to the great joy of Christ.
Try this: Say thank you in all sorts of ways on Christmas Eve and
Christmas Day.

The words spoken to the shepherds two thousand years ago were not
for them alone. . . . This is no old story that is relived once a year in
dusty memory, in colorful preparation, or in the fragrance of
evegreen and cinnamon. It is a living story calling you to enter into it
again and to receive the gift, tagged with your name. . . . We are
gifted by God with grace, new beginnings, and a promise of eternal
hope, and we are called to live fully and abundantly in this moment.
—Rob Weber, Where Heaven Touches Earth

Through the years, I have found myself wondering what it would have been like to be one of the "reporters" on the scene that night that Christ was born. Perhaps it is because I spent nearly three decades as a journalist and love to hear and tell good stories. But maybe it is because there is such pure joy resounding in the story of Christ's birth—joy that revolves around ordinary people, just like us. The news of the Lord's birth was given to shepherds who lived and worked in fields. Not unexpectedly, they were scared to death when an angel appeared to them. I have no doubt that I would have done my share of trembling had I been covering that story on that night.

The angel brought wonderful news, news for *all* people. The Savior was born for each of us—Christ, the Lord. That is the message that brings us right into Christmas Eve and Christmas Day. The story transcends whatever the world has done to the meaning of these particular days. By embracing the story afresh, we can claim these as special, holy holidays, reminded to look beyond our fear for the great joy that is possible.

Christmas Eve and Christmas Day bring such a mixture of emotions and activities, but we need to focus on the message of that announcement—a Savior for *all*. God gives us the gift of these days; it is up to us to give ourselves the gift of enjoying them, trying to turn any negative thoughts into thoughts of thanksgiving and praise, focusing not on what is unimportant but on the truly important things taking place.

I think back to my childhood, when my little brother and I anticipated Christmas Eve with such excitement that sometimes it felt as though my heart would leap out of my chest. I recall the connection I always felt on Christmas Eve and Christmas, knowing that my path would cross that of family and friends. Even though my family was quite poor, we always had a special Christmas Eve meal and always had pres-

GOD GIVES US THE GIFT OF THESE DAYS; IT IS UP TO US TO GIVE OURSELVES THE GIFT OF ENJOYING THEM.

ents under the tree and stockings filled with small goodies.

As I have aged, I still look forward to the sparkle that somehow decorates these days, even when they may not be picture perfect or go quite as I had imagined. Many of the people I encounter have mixed feelings about December 24 and 25. Some folks are filled with happiness, some with sadness. Some people have the joy of being with loved ones; others, the loneliness of being away; some, the pleasure of giving a special gift or the pain of having little. For many there is a blend of excitement and relief, a combination of knowing this is a very special time and being glad that it is almost over.

In the same way that we needed to step back and assess the days leading up to December 24 and 25, we need to be careful about how we approach the days themselves. We need to avoid, as my friend Craig says, building them into "some sort of perfect magical time," because that will likely lead to disappointment. In addition, in working with groups, I sometimes hear from those who let themselves feel like victims when the actual days roll around—feeling taken for granted or unappreciated.

These days are good days to give with love and not in expectation of what will be given in return, days to provide food and festivities out of kindness and not obligation.

Approaching Christmas Eve and Christmas Day committed to having a calm, happy spirit can make all the difference. This positive attitude is a gift you can give yourself—something no one else can deliver for you.

Celebrations Vary

The ways in which people celebrate and worship and connect on these two days vary widely. Asking people to talk about what is special in their family usually results in a flood of stories and memories and small things done in special ways again and again. For some, Christmas Eve is the true day of merrymaking. For others, Christmas Day draws the family together into large gatherings full of food and fun.

Worship is included for many, that sweet time of community when hearts and voices are lifted to God in praise, a moment of stillness that occurs despite the busyness of the days leading up to it. For many, attending church is the foundation of Christmas Eve—the last candle is lit on the Advent wreath, and in joyful awe the congregation sings of what happened that holy night.

My friend Birdie has found Christmas Eve worship to be especially important in recent years. "In early December, we block out the afternoon and evening of Christmas Eve on our calendars, because we are communion stewards and know that our obligations will fall somewhere in there. That way, no matter when our various sets of kids decide to come to worship, we can be with them. That is our priority now."

Christmas Eve is the day it all comes together, one way or the other. What is not done will not get done. What is done is just right. If it is a workday, the pace is a bit slower, even in retail centers. A sense of goodwill seems to seep into the most unlikely places.

My friend Kathie's family is among those who hang onto an old Southern tradition of saying "Christmas Eve gift" first to someone on December 24. "In my family, we play strictly for bragging rights. No gifts involved. It sounds silly but it's a big part of what makes our family Christmas." Another friend describes a similar tradition: "When we call family on Christmas Eve morning, we say, 'Christmas Eve gift.' And many in my family say that instead of hello when they answer the phone. My mother *always* answered the phone with that phrase on Christmas Eve."

As December 24 draws to a close and families and friends begin to gather, traditions of all sorts play out. One grandmother says a nativity scene is a key part of their celebration: "We have several small, children-friendly nativity scenes they play with and one large ceramic white one that is the focal point of the living room. We never place the baby Jesus in the manger until Christmas Eve after the worship services." That honor goes to the youngest child present.

Sometimes Christmas Eve traditions are affected by unforeseen circumstances, such as my elementary school friend Karen's story about a Louisiana ice storm in the late 1990s. Tradition called for a get-together with her husband's family on Christmas Eve, but most relatives were without electricity. So, at the last minute the gathering moved to my friend's house. "Well, I had no food, refreshments, nothing along the lines of a party. Luckily my house was pretty clean. We got barbecue and soft drinks, and we all had the best time. My mother-in-law always makes what we call her 'famous eggnog,' which was about the only thing that was prepared before the party, but when my husband picked it up at her house, he slipped on the ice on her steps and the whole thing spilled. He wasn't hurt except for his pride. Of course, we remind him of this now at the annual Christmas Eve celebrations. That was a memorable Christmas Eve, and one we all still talk about and smile over."

My friend Althea says that the quiet on Christmas Eve after the hubbub is over is almost holy; she savors it. Her observation inspires me to pause in the evening and welcome Christ in the quiet stillness after so many days of activity.

The Richness of Christmas Day

Christmas Day is a rare time when the world slows down. Many stores and restaurants are closed. Public activities are few. Traffic is lighter. People take a deep breath and move into personal activities that have meaning to them—whether a fancy meal or staying in their pajamas all day.

Missy, a woman I first met at church in Florida, says her family has a very particular way to celebrate. "On Christmas Eve we have an early casual dinner, sometimes with friends or family, and then go to the Christmas Eve candlelight service at the church. We leave out cookies and milk for Santa. After the kids go to bed, we add baby Jesus to the nativity scene. On Christmas morning we take our time opening gifts. This was very difficult when the kids were little, but over the years we have seen a real difference as they have truly learned to appreciate the gifts they've received and to enjoy sharing others' excitement as they open their gifts. Christmas Day dinner is always spaghetti and meatballs, which my husband prepares, and a birthday cake for Jesus, which we bake together in the afternoon."

My friend Mary D. says that chicken gumbo is part of her Christmas celebration. "My father died when I was fifteen. We had a farm to run, and my mother worked outside of the home. She was busy from sunup to sundown and then some. She loved entertaining, and holidays were always held at our old farmhouse. It wasn't until years later that I realized how difficult all of this had to be for her, although holidays were always joyful and meaningful. It truly didn't matter to her how many folks showed up for a holiday meal; there was always plenty to go around. My mother used what she had—chickens. She was known for creating her own recipes. Her chicken gumbo took no time to make, and you could stretch it if you had to, but most of all it was cheap and tasted great. We still make a pot of chicken gumbo every Christmas!"

Turning Again to the Christmas Story

The richness of this day is not to be taken for granted, whatever our circumstances.

Some years, perhaps your Christmas Day finds you separated from those you love or feeling blue. Or maybe you are worn out and sad because you did not slow down as you had intended. Use this day for prayer and reading the Christmas story in the Bible. Consider how God's promises are fulfilled, over and over again, not only in Bible stories but in our lives. You might ponder the story of Mary, who was chosen to be used by God:

> "Blessed is she who has believed that what the Lord has said to her will be accomplished!" And Mary said: "My soul glorifies the Lord and my spirit rejoices in God my Savior, for he has been mindful of the humble state of his servant." (Luke 1:45-48)

These words remind us that God uses ordinary people to serve, and this day is a perfect day for committing to believe and be of use, to listen and respond.

Or turn again to the transforming words in Luke 2. They are worth reading again and again, especially in a quiet moment on Christmas Day, a story shared at that moment between you and your loving God:

> And there were shepherds living out in the fields nearby, keeping watch over their flocks at night. An angel of the Lord appeared to them, and the glory of the Lord shone around them, and they were terrified. But the angel said to them, "Do not be afraid. I bring you good news of great joy that will be for all the people. Today in the town of David a Savior has been born to you; he is Christ the Lord." (Luke 2:8-11)

As Christmas draws to a close, may you be touched by Immanuel, Messiah, Comforter, God with us. Through this season may you be reminded that Jesus came, comes still, will come again.

Simple Tips from Friends

Turn to the Bible.

"I usually go to my mother's home for Christmas. We wake up (really early) and read the Christmas story from the Bible—from not one account but two, Matthew and Luke. It's a good reminder, before getting lost in the excitement of the day, of what the occasion is all about."

Talk to each other.

"Think and talk with your spouse, partner, or friend about the meaning of the holiday. Is Christmas about buying gifts and going to parties? Or is it first and foremost about celebrating the gift of God's Son?"

Be flexible.

"Don't let bumps in the road or changes in plans dampen your holiday cheer. Remind yourself of the reason for the season, pray for patience and peace, and keep your focus."

CHAPTER NINE

Hello, New Year

Setting Goals to Start the Year with Optimism

*Take heart: You can accomplish amazing things
by calling upon God's power.
Try this: Set bold goals for the year ahead.*

*Now to him who is able to do immeasurably more than
all we ask or imagine, according to his power that is at
work within us, to him be glory in the church and in
Christ Jesus throughout all generations, for ever and ever!*
—Ephesians 3:20

When we moved into our home a couple of years ago, there
was a large banana plant on the side of the house. Taller

than head high, it had beautiful purplish-pink blooms on it. In a yard that needed quite a lot of work, it was a sight to behold. About Thanksgiving time, however, freezing weather hit, and the plant withered. The beautiful green fronds and blooms became a big brown blob, ugly and depressing to look at. Finally, unable to bear the blight any longer, we cut it back to the ground.

In the spring, as other plants and flowers began to perk up, that plant looked incredibly sad. We began to consider what to plant in its place—and to dread digging up its huge root system.

Then one day a tiny green shoot popped up, then another. The shoots were minuscule, but they were alive. We decided to wait to see what might happen. Over the next few days, the plant nearly leaped from the ground. And, of course, within a few months the beautiful blooms appeared again. The giant plant was back in all its glory.

That stunning plant reminded me that it had a cycle to go through, that certain things needed to happen for it to do what it was created to do. I am hopeful now when it dies away in the winter that it will bloom again in the spring. Such is the way our lives are, which is one of the reasons I so look forward to the beginning of a new year. After Thanksgiving is gone (even the frozen turkey soup has been eaten) and Christmas celebrations are over, a wonderful new start comes.

Sometimes this great beginning is clouded by expectations of a magical New Year's Eve, a night that for many people fails to live up to its image and sours the notion of hope. This need not be the case. Choose a celebration that works for you—and do not feel compelled to stay up until the wee hours. You might choose a family fun night or a neighborhood potluck or a fancy party. You can decide to be with a crowd, with a few people, or alone. Remember to relax and do what you enjoy.

One of my best New Year's Eves ever was one I chose to spend alone when I was single. I rented a movie, grilled a steak, and went to bed early. My client Karen S. focuses on New Year's Day and what has become her favorite tradition: "Since 2000, the family and a few special invitees get together on New Year's Day and bike, walk, or run."

The Amazing Months Ahead

Once the festivities are over, move with joy into the New Year. Have you ever stopped to consider what amazing things twelve new months might bring? By taking simple steps, you can begin to shape the months ahead with hope and optimism. Life has taught us that we cannot control everything that happens to us. But we can control lots of it, and we can control how we react to everything.

My dream is that as you read this, you will have a much better sense of what you want to focus on in the year ahead, of things you want to do, of how to get started and how to follow up. These ideas work anytime, of course; if you do not get going at the first of a year, plunge in when you can, such as on your birthday or at the beginning of a new season.

Consider your perspective—how you approach the year and how you approach life overall. Begin to look for the good in life and to expect things to go right. Take time to step back and

assess what you want, knowing that God has wonderful plans for you and wants good things for you.

In our busy lives, it is difficult to find time to do this, but the rewards are worth the effort. Perhaps you will set aside a morning to ponder and plan and pray. Or, maybe you will take a day off from work. Perhaps you will curl up in a favorite chair one evening after work with a cup of hot chocolate, a candle burning, and a do-not-disturb-except-in-emergency sign for your family.

I love Saturday mornings. In my own life I've learned to set them aside in order to reflect, write, read something meaningful, make lists, consider decisions, critique some aspect of my life—you name it. This approach has helped me in setting goals, planning, figuring out what I want my life to look like, and then coming up with ways to make it happen. A vital part of this process is praying, listening to God's voice, trying to understand what the Creator wants me to do. Amazingly, by spending just a few minutes doing this each week, I often feel totally renewed.

If you are intimidated by the word goal (after all, it is a four-letter word), you might want to use the term *dream* or plan. Too often, people turn the goal-setting process into a chore or something that is not fun, rather than seeing it as an invigorating way to change our lives for the better.

For quite a few years I have stopped at the first of each year to take a fresh look at my life and work. I need to make sure I am still centered, doing my best to follow God's path for my life, living up to my beliefs. This planning process will be different for each of us. The form it takes will depend on our individual lives, our hopes and dreams, the needs we experience in our daily lives, and what we believe God is saying to us.

But some of the threads are the same.

First the What

Once again, start with the *what*. Then move on to the *how*. Decide what you want to accomplish. These can be big goals (get a college degree, start a business), medium-sized goals (lose ten pounds before class reunion), or small goals (fix a scratch on your car). You may want to shape your life and take more control. You may have a fitness goal. (I always find myself wanting to exercise more consistently, eat more healthfully, and—ahem—lose a few pounds.) You may want to do a major overhaul. You may want to focus on professional development and career movement, or on personal goals. You may want to develop a closer walk with God.

The process of assessing and planning can work for anyone. It helped me go from not being able to run a mile to running two marathons at the age of forty. It helped me start a successful part-time antique business as an entrepreneurial experiment. It helped me develop and implement a strategy for leaving my career as a journalist and starting a profitable consulting business.

As you list your goals, keep in mind the following:

Take into account the roles you play in your everyday life. I, for example, am a wife, friend, business owner, stepmom, grand-mother, sister, church member, civic club member, and writer. My life would be lopsided if I didn't consider all these roles. I can't realistically expect to improve in each of these areas in one year, so I must select priorities. I highly recommend that your spiritual life be high on the list because it will affect every other part of your life.

If you work outside the home or own a business, you may want to include a professional goal. Most people these days work to earn a living, and that takes an enormous part of our lives. Therefore, it is essential that we find work that is meaningful, if we are to enjoy each day to the fullest.

Since you can't do everything, focus on what is most important to you. What we focus on is generally what we get in life. I might talk for months about writing a book, but if I do not set a goal, come up with a topic, and schedule writing time, it will not happen. When I focus, I begin to make it happen. I find this in every area of my life. If I want to be more involved and more of a servant in my church, I must focus on that and consider ways to serve. I must be alert when opportunities come along. I must volunteer. If I want to lose ten (OK, or twenty) pounds, I must plan for exercise time and keep track of how many hot fudge sundaes I eat.

Decide on the areas of your life that you want to focus on. Perhaps they will be home and family, work, church, and spiritual growth. Maybe they will be financial, fun, fitness, and the future. One year, for example, my focus was on self-care (especially exercise), my spiritual life (prayer), my business (writing), and my closest personal relationships (home).

When you are pondering what God might want you to do in a new year, remember to plan for fun. We are created to enjoy life—and a good look around shows how much God has given us to enable us to do so. I realize more and more that we must seize each day for its joy and blessings. You can plan for fun by setting some goals and beginning to take even small steps. You'll be amazed by year-end at how far you have come. Pat, who helps run a family business, has tried to set goals for "semi-retirement," taking brief little breaks. "I felt very strongly that I needed some fun things to do for myself, so that I could be easier to live with and enjoy life more," she says. "I played golf, did errands, ate lunch with girlfriends, slept in later in the mornings, cooked dinner for my husband, exercised more, and felt wonderful." When she didn't stay focused, she wound up working more and more. "I need to look at that particular goal again and work on it," she says, "empowering others in the office and giving myself that freedom to enjoy each day more!"

Once you have decided what you want to focus on in your life, write down your goals. Begin to pray about them. Something amazing happens when you begin to think about how your life might look, when you write down those goals and when you turn these hopes and dreams over to God.

Then the How

After we have figured out where we are going, then we figure out how to get there. To help make your goals and dreams come true, set aside some time through the year for follow-up. If you write down the goals and do not pick them up again until next December 31, you will find—oddly—that you probably will have accomplished some of them, because they have been in your mind and on paper. But you will accomplish far more if you check on them regularly.

Some goals can be accomplished fairly quickly as the year starts.

Perhaps your goal is to be more organized. (This seems to be a goal for lots of people I encounter at seminars.) So you decide that as the year starts, within the first two months, you will clean out your closet, organize your bill-paying system, and start a file to hold receipts for next year's taxes.

If your goal is more long-term, such as being committed to getting in shape, you will need consistent steps and follow-up. You might decide that you will exercise for at least thirty minutes four times a week. To see if you are sticking to this decision, you will need a system for keeping track of it, such as putting a sticker on your calendar for each day you exercised as planned.

Be specific!

The more specific you can be with your goals, the better. Instead of saying, "I'm going to be a better spouse," consider what you really are saying. Do you need to make more time to do enjoyable, relaxing activities with your husband or wife? Do you need to listen better at the end of each day? Do you need to be more encouraging as your spouse heads out the door each morning? Do you need to schedule a weekly date night when you go out to eat and see a movie? Or do you need to do something nice for your spouse by taking over some chore that he or she hates to do, such as pick up the dry cleaning or take out the trash?

Perhaps your vague goal is "to enjoy work more." Does that mean getting to work on time and making every effort to leave on time? Does it mean not getting into complaint sessions with co-workers, talks that are draining and time-consuming and accomplish little? Does it mean beginning to look for another job more suited to your skills?

Make a timeline for when you want to accomplish each of the goals. Set realistic deadlines for each item. Decide if you can do a few of the smaller, less time-consuming goals fairly quickly and get them off the list.

Break larger goals into steps. What specifically do you need to do to accomplish that particular goal? Begin systematically to work through the steps. Sometimes this process may seem daunting. But most of us have the skills to do this. We have years of practice getting things done—lots of things. We handle homes and jobs and the logistics of life. We make sure that the bills are paid and the children fed, and we do lots of extras in between. So, focusing on the year ahead and coming up with the steps we will take merely utilizes skills we have honed for years.

Consider having a special journal or notebook in which you keep track of these goals. A dedicated journal writer, I set aside a "Big Picture" notebook or journal. Although I am not really an artist, I draw, cut things out of magazines, use colored pens and pencils, and try to be open to possibilities. This sounds a bit corny but it is amazing how it helps me sort out my ideas and crystallize my thinking about what I want to try, what I feel led to do, what I am shooting for in the months ahead.

Looking Back

As part of looking forward each year, I also take at least a few minutes to look back, assessing what worked and what didn't.

What did I accomplish in the past year? What am I proud of? What blessings surrounded me? What were my biggest disappointments? What did I not do that I planned to or hoped to? Where did I heed the nudge of God?

Looking back is somewhat difficult when we want to be looking ahead. But taking at least a quick look back can help us learn from our disappointments and mistakes. Then we can put them aside and move on. This works well to help us figure out what holds us back each year—roadblocks, speed bumps, detours. These can be nagging problems we never quite settle, personality traits we want to work on (such as being a better listener or trying to become more patient), or ways we procrastinate. By identifying these items, we can plan how to deal with them and move on. Bravely decide to take the steps necessary to move forward.

While identifying roadblocks and obstacles, also take some time to consider keys that will help. Two of the best are prayer and the Bible.

I try to saturate my plans in prayer, and I often turn to the Bible—sometimes in near desperation—for how I am to live or what I am to do. These tools keep me more in tune with what God wants, rather than having me go off on tangents. And they remind me that the day really belongs to God. My purpose is to serve and to love and to live abundantly: "For it is by grace you have been saved, through faith—and this not from yourselves, it is the gift of God—not by works, so that no one can boast. For we are God's workmanship, created in Christ Jesus to do good works, which God prepared in advance for us to do" (Ephesians 2:8-10).

Another key is information. Moving forward is often a matter of learning something. When I decided I wanted to start a business, I had a list of strategies that included reading about business, talking with people in business, asking for advice from friends and family. I had to learn how to write a business plan and find out what legal steps were needed.

Another key is the calendar. The only way I can achieve my goals and live the life I long for is to make sure I spend my time on my top priorities. For example, one of my goals is to be a loving grandmother. To narrow down that goal, I decided I would spend more time with my young granddaughter, I would pray for her daily, and I would look for ways to let her know I'm thinking of her. To make sure this happens, I try to schedule in advance blocks of time to spend with her, making arrangements for her to come down for a week in the spring, again in the summer, and again at Thanksgiving. When I travel for work or pleasure, I send her postcards. (I admit this has had a downside. She thinks I work on an airplane.)

Still another key is money. If you dream of going to Italy for two weeks, you will probably have to plan and save. If you want to join a gym to meet your fitness goal, you may have to cut out another expense.

When you set your goals, dream big.

Many of my clients—and myself, too—tend to think too small. We think of reasons we can't do something instead of reasons we can or what we might do.

Take your Big Picture thinking to Bigger Picture.

I have come to believe that we can do almost anything if we

set our mind to it, focus on it, take action. When you start this, you don't know where you'll wind up. You might find yourself, as I did, owning a wonderful little antique store in a fishing village in Florida. You might open a new business or run a marathon. You could write a book or take a leadership position at church. You might line up for that promotion at work.

If some of your biggest dreams could come true in the year ahead or the next few years, what might they be? Take your journal or notebook or the back of an envelope and begin listing those dreams. Do not edit yourself or hold back. Mine, by the way, include being a best-selling author who helps people hurry and worry less. I dream of living a peaceful, contented, relaxed life. I want to travel to many interesting and unusual places with my husband. This dream includes a leisurely trip around the world one of these days. Before that, I want to spend a summer in a lovely location writing a novel that has been in my mind and notebooks for several years now.

Big, wonderful dreams are very individualized, and they depend on our perspective. A friend wants to own a vacation home in a cooler climate, surrounded by friends in similar cabins. Another friend would love to move with her family to a farm. A client wants to retire from her job and make a difference in the community. Another client wants to develop a national program to help children in need express themselves through writing and telling their stories.

Without dreaming about the things we want to do and then focusing on the steps to do them, we will not be as likely to reach our goals. The days will continue to fly by, as they are prone to do, and we will be full of regrets and "if onlys" instead of "what ifs." As you live each day in the year ahead, focus on your goals and your dreams: Give thanks every day. Hurry less. Worry less. Enjoy each day.

Dream big and do it! Whatever hap-

> DREAM BIG AND DO IT! WHATEVER HAPPENS, CONTINUE MOVING FORWARD WITH JOY, TRUSTING GOD TO WALK WITH YOU IN THE YEAR AHEAD.

pens, continue moving forward with joy, trusting God to walk with you in the year ahead.

Simple Tips from Friends

Recall the good things of the past.

"I love reflecting over the past year's joys and over the people who have brought me many blessings—reflecting on how God has blessed me!"

Pray for others.

"Every New Year I make a prayer list, with someone at the top whom I am going to pray for. It may be someone who hasn't been converted or someone who is going through great difficulties. I make it a point to remember to praise and thank God before asking for things!"

Set goals and follow up on them.

"When I think of goals daily, I am so good about following them. If I don't, then I tend to veer in a million different directions and definitely don't accomplish much. Journaling helps keep me true to my goals. When I think it and write it down, it happens!"

CHAPTER TEN

Growing Stronger Spiritually

Using the Days Until Epiphany

*Take heart: God is on this journey with you and
wants you to live abundantly, fully.
Try this: Choose a gift you will give back to God in the year ahead.*

*Restore to me the joy of your salvation and grant
me a willing spirit, to sustain me.*
—Psalm 51:12

By New Year's Day, most of us are ready to say farewell to the Christmas season. A little college football and a helping of black-eyed peas—perhaps a bit of order restored to the holiday clutter—and it is time to move away from the holidays and into the busy routine of everyday life. We often breathe a sigh of relief, as though we have crossed the finish line in a race and can now catch our breath. But the holiness of the Christmas season does not end on December 26. It extends until January 6, Epiphany, a day that commemorates the birth of Jesus, the visit of the Magi, and Jesus' baptism.

As the story is told in the Bible: "After Jesus was born in Bethlehem in Judea, during the time of King Herod, Magi from the east came to Jerusalem and asked, 'Where is the one who has been born king of the Jews? We saw his star in the east and have come to worship him'" (Matthew 2:1-2).

The Magi were likely men of science of some sort, perhaps astrologers, and they clearly believed this was no ordinary star. On their journey, they were secretly called to meet with King Herod, who was afraid (and likely jealous) of the birth of this new king. Like so many things that threaten to draw us off course in life, Herod was deceptive. He asked the Magi to find the child and let him know, so that he, too, could worship Jesus. Of course, the likelihood was that he wanted to harm the child.

The wise men continued to follow the star. "On coming to the house, they saw the child with his mother Mary, and they bowed down and worshiped him. Then they opened their treasures and presented him with gifts of gold and of incense and myrrh" (Matthew 2:11). They were taking a risk for Christ, believing they had to worship him, even though the king would not like it.

Does this passage speak to you? Is God calling you to take a chance or step out for a special purpose?

As we move from Christmas to Epiphany and into the year ahead, perhaps it is time to leave our comfort zone to do some-thing different—at work, in the community, at church, or in our relationships.

Christmas and Easter, sacred holidays in the Christian tra-dition, have become part of our secular culture. Epiphany, by contrast, is not well known. (In my informal survey, most peo-ple knew virtually nothing about Epiphany other than, "It's in early January and has something to do with the Magi.") The days between Christmas and Epiphany offer us a fine time to consider a new approach to our spiritual life and the kind of person we want to be. Epiphany is not just a "P.S." to the hol-idays. It is a special Christian holiday that continues to cele-brate the birth of Christ, not limiting it to one day of consumption and chaos.

Maybe we can imagine ourselves as modern-day Magi, seek-ing Christ, wanting to give something to Jesus, being willing to take a risk for him.

With all the noise of the world and the busy-ness of life, it is difficult to pay attention to our spiritual lives, that part of us that yearns to *do less* and *be more*, to serve more faithfully, to feel as though we are responding in the way God would have us respond. But the days leading up to Epiphany can provide just such a framework, a time to consider how we will grow with God in the year ahead. Through our example, we can shape these two weeks into something precious for those around us, showing that the joy of Christ does not end after the celebration of his birth on Christmas Day.

A Time to Look Inward

The days leading up to Epiphany provide a special, spiritual time to look inward and to reflect upon what Christ means in our lives. These few days are a wonderful time to pray about how to hear God and how to be strong enough to act on God's call for us. Consider meditating on the words of Psalm 131:2: "I have stilled and quieted my soul." Starting the year with a still and quiet soul could be an unparalled blessing in our busy world.

Interestingly, the word *epiphany* also means a sudden perception of the meaning of something or a simple and striking grasp of something. It means a moment when something is made clear, illuminated, or revealed to us. It is an "aha" moment in our lives.

A year ago, I had such a moment after a very disturbing dream on two nights in the same week. I dreamed that I was at an airport and was nearly blind, could barely find my way around, and missed my plane. I had been praying that week about God's plan for my life. I awoke from those dreams certain that God's message was there for me—that I was not seeing clearly something that I needed to see. I began to pray that God would open my eyes, clear my mind, and help me understand the best next step for my life.

As the New Year starts and we move to Epiphany, consider the wise men who visited Christ, led by a star. They were clear in their vision, following the path laid out for them. Perhaps if we carry our focused spiritual direction beyond Christmas, into Epiphany, and beyond, we might suddenly grasp new ways to experience and share God's love and plans for our lives. For example, we might turn to Romans 8:26: "The Spirit helps us in our weakness. We do not know what we ought to pray for, but the Spirit himself intercedes for us with groans that words cannot express." We might enter the next twelve months with the certainty that the Holy Spirit is with us and can help us even when we do not know how to pray.

As you have worked your way through the pages of this book, you have been asked to consider what you want your holiday season to look like. You have, perhaps, found ways to give thanks and to live with a grateful spirit. You have struggled to slow down during the fast pace of Christmas and to celebrate the birth of Christ again, just as you might celebrate the birth of a beloved new child in your family. You have been offered tools to help you set goals and dream about the year ahead and how to shape a life you long for, to enjoy each day more.

Consider using Epiphany as a season to consider how you can grow into more of the person God wants you to be, how you can live your life with a magnificence that will only come from sincerely seeking first God's kingdom. Perhaps these days, between December 25 and January 6, can become a time of spiritual introspection and growth during which you contemplate how to seek and do God's good, perfect, and pleasing will (as described in Romans 12:2).

If you allow God to guide you through these weeks, they can offer a spiritual foundation to lead you into and through the year with God's grace surrounding you and heavenly mercy guiding you. What is especially wonderful about pausing during these few days is that they come after what is traditionally one of the most

HOW WOULD YOUR LIFE LOOK IF YOU FOLLOWED GOD EACH AND EVERY DAY?

hectic times of the year. Perhaps a personal, spiritual focus can offer just what you need to go joyfully into the days ahead.

Moving Forward

Gary Spencer, a Florida pastor and mentor, uses a baseball analogy to talk about our development as believers. Gary's fervent wish is that each of us might continue to grow, in essence hitting a spiritual home run, getting to where God wants us to be. He stresses that this growth process involves being part of the church community and giving.

If you are a mature Christian, as Epiphany approaches perhaps you will delve more deeply into God's word or pray for new insights that will move you further along in your faith. If you are a seeker or new believer, maybe you will take small steps to go to the next base. This spiritual focus will fit well with the goal setting and dreaming we talked about in the previous chapter. It can, in fact, help shape your goals and dreams. But it goes much deeper. It helps you decide how you will greet each day, live the day, and end the day. How would your life look if you followed God each and every day?

The period between Christmas and Epiphany is a good time to see if we are still in the game, if we are indeed moving around the bases or if we have decided to sit on the bench. As you get back into a routine and the year starts and work begins again and school starts back up, commit that you will spend some time each day studying and listening for God's help.

This commitment starts with prayer.

Prayer might mean sitting down in the morning and writing out how you want to live in the day ahead. It might mean asking God throughout the day to direct your thoughts and steps. It might mean asking before you sleep that God will speak to you and that you will hear. My sister-in-law Mary Frances, a retiree from the healthcare business and a church volunteer, feels strongly about developing the habit of prayer in order to grow spiritually: "Prayer is powerful in two ways—going up to God in praise and obedience, and in the benefits that come down to us providentially. We don't always see the results of prayer, but many times we know prayer was answered. We may think things that happen are circumstantial, but if we believe, we know that God's providence is carried out in many instances."

The Bible is the next resource on this journey.

You might pick a passage of Scripture and reflect on parts of it each day. For example, you might choose the wonderful words of Philippians mentioned earlier:

> Rejoice in the Lord always. I will say it again: Rejoice! Let your gentleness be evident to all. The Lord is near. Do not be anxious about anything, but in everything, by prayer and petition, with thanksgiving, present your requests to God. And the peace of God, which transcends all understanding, will guard your hearts and your minds in Christ Jesus.
> Finally, brothers, whatever is true, whatever is noble, whatever is right, whatever is pure, whatever is lovely, whatever is

admirable—if anything is excellent or praiseworthy—think about such things. Whatever you have learned or received or heard from me, or seen in me—put it into practice. *And the God of peace will be with you.* (Philippians 4:4-9; italics mine)

Consider what Paul's advice to the Philippians might mean in your daily life. How can it help you become a better person, a person living your calling? Think about choosing one idea from these verses to focus on each day for two weeks:

At-a-glance reminder:
1. Give thanks.
2. Be kind to others.
3. Don't worry about anything—instead pray about everything.
4. Think good thoughts.
5. Put God's teachings into practice.
6. Expect God's peace.

Another way to make use of the Bible is to choose a scripture each day, write it down, and pray about its meaning in your life. Perhaps you would choose the reminder from Hebrews: "Now faith is being sure of what we hope for and certain of what we do not see" (Hebrews 11:1). You might ask God to strengthen your faith in the year ahead and to forgive your sins. Perhaps you will consider ways that your faith has been tested and ways it has grown.

Or you could use this unique period between Christmas and Epiphany to consider how you can best serve God in the year ahead. What are the best next steps you can take? Were you faithful and committed in the year just past? Do you need to make adjustments in your spiritual life?

Many of us are overwhelmed after the holidays, feeling as though we have overspent, overeaten, overscheduled. We might use this time to consider how to be better stewards of our money and time in the year ahead, reading Luke 12:48b: "From everyone who has been given much, much will be demanded; and from the one who has been entrusted with much, much more will be asked."

An Ongoing Process

Shaping our spiritual life is an ongoing process. I compare it to the bonsai trees that my husband grows. They require frequent pruning (branches *and* roots) and lots of water and care. Some also need fairly forceful reshaping. My husband says that bonsai trees are just like us—the younger they are, the more easily they are shaped; the older they are, the harder it gets. As we age and mature as Christians, sometimes we become stiff and unbending. This time of reflection can help us yield to God's shaping.

In my spiritual life, I find myself sometimes as certain as can be and at other times floundering, hoping for a word or sign that might settle me down and put me squarely on the right path. Using my pastor friend's analogy, I am like the base runner who wants to steal second but keeps returning to first base, afraid of moving on. I often recall the words of the apostle Paul: "I do not understand what I do. For what I want to do I do not do, but what I hate I do" (Romans 7:15).

One approach to Epiphany is to pray for discernment about changes you need to make in what you do and do not do. Perhaps you need to become more consistent in your church attendance. Or maybe you need to attend a Bible study or connect with a small group. Maybe you need to stop doing something you are doing—whatever is keeping you from being the person God wants you to be.

Live with Joy

Return to the words of the Psalmist at the beginning of this chapter: "Restore to me the joy of your salvation and grant me a *willing* spirit, to sustain me" (Psalm 51:12; italics mine).

As you contemplate being a child of God who lives abundantly in Christ, remember these simple steps to living each day with more joy:

Make up your mind to enjoy each day. Don't worry about yesterday. Don't fret about tomorrow. Enjoy today!
Pray for God's guidance and blessings.
Hurry less. Slow it down!
Worry less. Be anxious for nothing!
See the best in each situation, for each person. Be thankful for the good instead of focusing on the bad.
Give thanks each day.
Simplify your plans.
Help others.
Enjoy nature. Get outside more often. Learn from the seasons.

Read the Bible regularly. Choose other inspirational materials to learn from.

Be a good steward of your time, talent, and finances.

Know that God has great plans for you. Christ came that you would have life to the full—abundant life, a wonderful, happy, contented life.

Finally, remember the Magi and the precious gifts they gave to Jesus, items that were of great value. Decide to give something back to God: perhaps some of your most precious gift, time, to help those in need, to teach a class at church, or to volunteer in your community. Remember that God will give you the power and wisdom to do what you are called to do. Maybe you will make a decision to give part of your income back to your church or to a worthy cause in the year ahead, knowing that "where your treasure is, there your heart will be also" (Matthew 6:21). Possibly your gift will be a gift of your heart, committing (or recommitting) to walking on the path where God would have you walk, spending more time quietly in the presence of the King who was born all those years ago—time in prayer, Bible study, reflection, and listening for the still, small voice.

May you believe that anything that can go right will go right and that God will provide you with great power. Peace and joy to you.

Simple Tips from Friends

Carry the spirit of Christmas into the year ahead and plan time for worship.

"Find a way to maintain that spirit all year long."

"As members of Jesus' body, we are completed when we worship together as one."

Learn from friends.

"It is as if I am drawn to people who are trying to learn and understand more. My dearest friends seem to be yearning for deeper spirituality, and we talk and learn from each other. I think that our lives are never-ending searches for what takes us to a deeper, more meaningful spiritual relationship with God."

Become part of a small group.

"I am finally in a small group (women's lunchtime group) that lives out Richard Foster's statement about the purpose of small groups—'to become better disciples of Jesus Christ.'"

Resources to Help You Along the Way

May you be blessed with many unhurried and unworried moments from Thanksgiving to Advent to Christmas to New Year's to Epiphany and beyond. And may you find others to walk with you along the way, knowing that the world is full of people seeking a calmer, more spiritual, more joyful Christmas season and a more hopeful way to live each day.

Consider Starting an Advent Group

In observing Advent, as with most things in life, the help of friends is a wonderful tool. Invite a group of people to meet each week during Advent to focus on the sweetness of Christ's birth as the world gets increasingly frantic, so that all of you can hurry less and worry less as you anticipate the birth of Christ.

Start a Devotional Journal

Pray about the scriptures mentioned in this book or others that you read during this season. Ask God to help you understand what they mean for your life and how you are to live.

Work with a Friend to Simplify the Season

Consider meeting for lunch or e-mailing once a week to talk about what is going on and what can be eliminated. Encourage each other. Hold each other accountable.

Reflect on These Questions, Alone or with a Small Group

What do you love about "the holidays"—the period from Thanksgiving through New Year's and into Epiphany?

What do you dislike or even dread about that season?

Do you have a favorite tradition? If so, describe it.

Do you have a tradition you'd like to change or get rid of? If so, explain.

What tips have you come up with that help you slow down and savor the holidays?

What have you learned about yourself during holidays of the past?

What might you do to grow spiritually in the New Year?

What goals might you set for the year ahead?

What nagging problems slow you down or draw you off course?

Make a Checklist to Keep Yourself Organized

Here are a few hints that might help liberate you from the tyranny of a frenzied commercial season that bears little resemblance to your heart's desire:

Keep a good calendar. Pull out the calendar in the early fall and begin to consider what you know will be coming up. For example, one of our challenges each year is to decide when we will go to Tennessee, my husband's home state. We usually go just before Christmas, allowing most folks to be back home for Christmas Eve and Christmas morning. My sister-in-law and I usually volley a few dates around via e-mail before we settle on one that works for everyone, built around job schedules, travel plans of others, and so forth. Starting early and making a plan eases this pressure tremendously. For those who travel by airplane, planning in advance is crucial to help get the best fares and available flights.

As soon as you know of other events you want to attend, put them on the calendar, too—from the Christmas program at your child's school to your office party to the cantata at church. Go ahead and pencil in dates you have in mind for anything extra, such as giving a party for the neighbors or your small group at church. Then stick with these events as much as possible, spending your time on what is most important. Use the calendar to help you say no to events that just do not fit in, even if they would be enjoyable. Remember: You cannot do everything.

Make a gift list and carry it with you. Write down the names of everyone you plan to give a gift to. Next to the names, jot down the gifts you plan to give them or have already bought them. This helps me immensely. It keeps me from overlooking someone I truly want to remember at Christmas, and it allows me to jot down a gift idea when it pops into my head.

Make a list of other things you want to do or consider doing. Compare this list with your calendar. This comparison will help you realize what you can get done without too much wear and tear on you. If every day is filled up with planned events, for example, when will you shop or wrap presents or spend time watching a holiday movie with the children or quietly remembering the real purpose of the season?

Make a timeline. If you really want to send photos with your Christmas cards, when will you have the pictures taken and processed? When do they need to go into the mail so that you are not rushing at the last minute? How much time will it take you to address the cards and write a note? By breaking down these tasks, even the fun ones, into bite-sized pieces, you not only get a clearer idea of how much time they will really take, but you also can decide if this is how you truly want to spend your time. I think here of a dear friend who decided one Christmas to make matching outfits for her five grandchildren. Not being a great seamstress, she put off the project until the last minute and became panicky over it. "What was I thinking?" she later said. "I had a full-time job, a teenager at home, and all that shopping to do. And our holidays were no merrier than they would have been without matching outfits."

Consult with your spouse or significant other before committing to holiday events. When one person says yes to this occasion and the other says yes to that, conflicts occur. Either activities pile up on the same day, or the pace of a given week gets out of hand.

Plan at-home time for being with your family or doing some of the odd jobs that must be done during this season. Write this time on your schedule. I know if I plan something for every evening (which is not hard to do as the holidays pick up), I will not have time to decorate the tree or write notes to friends or wrap gifts.

Plan spiritual time—church services and special holiday events, as well as quiet times to pray and reflect. Without our being conscious of it, the season can easily slip away without a focus on the most important aspects of all. I think of recent years when New Year's has fallen on a weekend—with the accompanying temptation to miss church. And then I think of the haunting beauty of singing "Amazing Grace" to the tune of "Auld Lang Syne" and the power of ending a year and starting afresh in worship.

Start a Christmas Journal

Some people believe that the perfect Christmas tree or just the right gift starts the Christmas season off right. For my friend Carol, it's pulling out her Christmas journal and making sure she has good lists.

A creative person, Carol wanted to do lots of things and do them all well. She is a loving person, so she regularly looks for people who need a special touch during the Christmas season. To top it off, she sends the most original card we get each year, clever and personal. She decorates her house and cooks lots of home-made goodies. (Yes, she serves beautiful meals on real china!) She combines her love of Christ and the spiritual side of the season with a fun social side, spending time with the people she cares about. Through the years, it sometimes became too much. By Christmas morning, she was worn out and discouraged. But no more.

Here is how she explained it in an excerpt from an essay she wrote:

> I have a strategic plan of my own, the objective of which is not just to survive, but enjoy Christmas. It's a plan born out of need, conceived amidst the shreds of ribbon and leftover turkey following last year's Christmas debacle, when I promised myself, "There will never be another year like this."
>
> First, I analyzed my problems: getting out my decorations so late that I was throwing them around the house in temporary locations never to be properly arranged; trying to make my purple wool look like a party dress; ironing my daughter's holiday dress five minutes before Christmas Eve church; providing nothing for my family to eat but rum balls and fudge; wrapping on Christmas Eve the packages that I'd bought in June; rushing to the post office to get our cards postmarked before December 25.
>
> I won't subject you to more of my shortcomings, but suffice to say the list goes on. So before my mood of self-debasement waned and my resolve weakened, I took out my new calendar and mapped out a schedule for the next Christmas, one guaranteed to bring me and my family to Christmas Eve in peace (or should I say "one piece"?) and harmony.

Let me hear from you!

I would love to hear about your journey and ways you have learned to hurry less and worry less, as well as tips for others and ongoing challenges. I also would welcome an opportunity to speak to your group, lead a retreat, or work with you as you try a new approach to life. Please e-mail me at judy@judychristie.com.

*A Sampling of Great Recipes,
Simple Tips, an Advent Study
for Individuals or Groups,
a Lesson for Epiphany,
& More!*

*You will go out in joy
and be led forth in peace.*
—Isaiah 55:12 NIV

Dear Readers:

What a delight to watch busy people move forward on a more joyful path at Christmas, energized and enriched!

Through the years since *Hurry Less, Worry Less at Christmas* was written, life seems to have gotten even noisier and more hectic— and I've taught (and studied) these hurry-less-worry-less ideas

131

many times. I've seen small changes make big differences in myself and others. As individuals are transformed, they affect those around them. The news of great joy takes hold in fresh ways.

In discussions and celebrations, I am reminded of how this time of year is meant to be special, not stressful. And I very much want to help you step back and take a fresh look, to shape the Christmas you long for. Be assured that it's possible to slow down and enjoy this season more. It starts with small steps, everyday decisions that change your attitude and your activities.

In Louisiana, we use the word *lagniappe* to mean "a little something extra." In the spirit of the season of giving, I hope you'll enjoy these extras in this edition of *Hurry Less, Worry Less at Christmas*. They've been chosen for you with love, prayer, and enthusiasm.

- A sampling of great recipes from friends and family
- Holiday how-to tips
- An Advent study that combines practical tips with Scriptures and questions for your life
- A lesson on Epiphany as we consider what we might offer to God in the New Year

Each year during Advent, I revisit ways to live more simply and celebrate God's gifts. I encourage you to do so also. Be transformed! Take a deep breath and decide to live differently. Pray about activities and ideas you want to get rid of and those you want to add.

Don't work so hard at making Christmas perfect. Instead, take a deep breath and enjoy its wonder. In the words of the prophet Isaiah: "Go out in joy and be led forth in peace"!

Special Recipes for Special Occasions

From Thanksgiving to Christmas, friends and family pull out prized recipes and offer the gift of cooking to people they love. Don't rush through your recipes, but consider who you're cooking for and savor the memories that old recipes evoke. Enjoy creating something special. These recipes have personal meaning in my life, and I'm excited to offer them to you. They were all created by cooks who are dear to me, and they are delicious!

Pretty Green Punch (named by my mother)

Each Christmas Eve, my mother liked to make punch, a sure sign that we were having a family party. Her old recipe, written in her own beautiful handwriting, is one of the things I treasure. This is a super simple recipe and popular with adults and children.

1 gallon lime sherbet
2 quarts ginger ale (chilled)
1 large can pineapple juice (chilled)

Mix all ingredients 30 minutes before serving. If you want a different color punch, simply change the flavor of the sherbet!

Easy Red and Green Christmastime Appetizer

My friend Carol and I met in the dorm during our first year of college. She has a knack for making special occasions extra special, and her inspiration is woven throughout Hurry Less, Worry Less at Christmas. She uses a journal to keep track of what works and what

*doesn't during the holiday season, and you'll find her journal sugges-
tions in "Resources to Help You Along the Way."*

*She also is a fantastic cook and offers one of her simple recipes here.
In Carol's words: "This is a really easy and pretty appetizer! You can
make it quickly and keep it in the refrigerator. I use it every Christmas.
It is great because it is red and green."*

Cranberry Jalapeño Relish

12-ounce package fresh cranberries
2-plus jalapeños, seeded and minced*
½ cup chopped cilantro
1 bunch green onions, chopped
¾ cup sugar
2 tablespoons oil
Juice of 1 lime

Chop cranberries, jalapeños, cilantro, and green onions sepa-
rately in the food processor until coarsely chopped. Stir together
all chopped ingredients with sugar, oil, and lime juice. Cover and
refrigerate several hours to allow flavors to blend. Serve over
cream cheese with crackers on the side. Also works well as a rel-
ish for ham and turkey.

*Because jalapeño peppers vary widely in heat, I usually start
with two peppers and then taste to see if more should be added.
Also, for those who do not like cilantro, substitute fresh mint. It
gives a totally different flavor.

Christmas Breakfast or Brunch

Ginger, a friend since eighth grade, is one of those hostesses who makes gathering around her antique family dining table a true joy. She likes to make breakfast or brunch casseroles the night before and cook them for holiday guests (or visitors any time of the year). These casseroles are delicious—and simple, even on mornings with lots going on.

G's Holiday Breakfast Casserole
1 pound country sausage, browned and drained
8 eggs
2 cups milk
8 ounces shredded cheddar cheese
6 slices bread, cubed
1 teaspoon dry mustard

Mix all ingredients and spread out in 9x13 casserole dish. Let sit overnight. Cook at 350 for 45 min. Let sit a few minutes before cutting. Great also as leftovers!

Here's an even easier recipe from Ginger.

Texas Eggs
3 8-ounce bags of shredded Jalapeño Jack cheese (1 or 2 of these can be plain Monterey Jack cheese)
6 eggs

Spread the cheese in a 9x13 baking pan. Beat the eggs and pour over the cheese. Bake for 30 min at 350. Cut into squares and serve.

Cooking for Love and Enjoyment

When longtime friend and coworker Kathie and I were young, neither of us cooked much. But as the years unfolded, I watched with awe as Kathie turned into a fantastic cook, making many old-fashioned Southern dishes and meals she'd eaten while growing up in Natchitoches Parish, Louisiana.

In Kathie's words: "I always loved my mother's cooking, but I was in my thirties before I realized why she went to so much trouble preparing food for her family. Then it hit me. It was her way of showing how much she loved us. I've inherited her enjoyment of cooking, and I strive to be half as good as she was."

Kathie wins top honors in potluck competitions in the newsroom where she works, and her sweet potato casserole is a crowd pleaser.

Kathie's Husband's Aunt's Praline Sweet Potatoes

3 cups sweet potatoes, cooked and mashed*

1 cup sugar

2 eggs

1 teaspoon vanilla

⅓ cup milk

½ cup margarine, melted

1 cup firmly packed brown sugar

⅓ cup all-purpose flour

⅓ cup margarine, melted

1 cup finely chopped pecans**

Combine sweet potatoes, sugar, eggs, vanilla, milk, and ½ cup margarine; beat with electric mixer until smooth. Spoon into a greased 2-qt. casserole dish. Combine brown sugar, flour, ⅓ cup margarine, and pecans; sprinkle over top of casserole. Bake at 350 degrees for 30 minutes.

*I usually use two medium-sized cans of sweet potatoes. Drain them well or it will be too soupy.

**I like pecans so if I have them I use a few more.

Traditions on the Table

When my family gathers for Thanksgiving dinner, certain dishes are always on the table, and I want to share them with you. I'd love to hear about your traditional family recipes, too. You can e-mail me at judy@judychristie.com.

Aunt Jean's Creamed Corn is prepared by my first-cousin Cindy, a recipe handed down from her mother. This is a fantastic dish, cooked on the top of the stove (handy since so many dishes require the oven). We always have fun visiting while one of us stirs!

Aunt Jean's Creamed Corn

2 bags frozen whole-kernel corn

1 stick butter

Salt (to taste)

Pepper (to taste)

Sugar (to taste)

Quart carton of half-and-half

Be sure to break up clumps of corn kernels. Use a food processor or blender if necessary. Don't turn them to mush, but break up the clumps. Put corn in skillet with stick of butter, salt, pepper, sugar, and half-and-half. Turn burner on low and cook for 30 minutes.

Jane's Cheese Potatoes

The following potato dish is so popular (and tasty) that my sister-in-law finds herself peeling lots of potatoes each year. As children have gotten married and visit different houses on Thanksgiving, they always make a request: "Save some of Aunt Jane's Cheese Potatoes for us!"

Approximately 10 medium potatoes
1 stick butter or margarine
1 cup milk
½ pint whipping cream
3 cups shredded cheddar cheese
Salt and pepper

Peel and cube potatoes. Boil them until a fork enters easily. Drain. Return to pan and add butter and milk. Mix well. Beat whipping cream to a high peak and fold into potatoes. Add half the cheese. Add salt and pepper to taste. Pour into a 9x13 casserole dish and spread remainder of cheese on top. Cook at 350 degrees for 20 to 30 minutes or until lightly brown.

Eva's Green Bean Casserole

One of my annual assignments is Green Bean Casserole, the one time of year our crew requests green beans. This recipe is from my mother-in-law.

1 package frozen French style green beans

1 can cream of mushroom soup

¼ cup water

¼ cup slivered almonds (optional)

Salt to taste

1 small can French fried onion rings

Cook beans per instructions on package. Place beans into an 8x8 casserole dish. Add soup, water, almonds, and salt. Cover and bake at 350 degrees for 45 minutes. For the last 15 minutes, uncover and add onion rings to top.

The Tradition of Chicken Gumbo for Christmas Dinner

When I interviewed friends and family about Christmas traditions, Mary D. told me about always making a pot of chicken gumbo on Christmas. (For more on traditions, see chapter 8.)

Mary says: "I never really wondered why we always had chicken gumbo for Christmas dinner* because that was what we were having—end of discussion. Now that I'm grown and have my share of Christmas dinners at my own house, I understand Mama's time-honored tradition. Since our farm house was always packed to overflowing with relatives and anyone else who happened to show up, her recipe was quick, easy, and inexpensive."

Mary's Mama's Chicken Gumbo

1 chicken, whole or boneless

½ cup flour

½ cup oil for roux
¼ cup oil for gumbo
2 cups chopped onion
2 cups chopped celery
Broth from boiling chicken plus 2 or 3 more cans
Salt and pepper

Boil chicken and cut up coarsely, removing bones and skin if using whole chicken. Reserve broth. Make a roux by browning ½ cup flour and ½ cup oil in a skillet.** Spoon this into a large soup pot. In the same skillet (no need to wash), add about ¼ cup more oil. Stir in onion and celery. Heat until they are soft, stirring occasionally. Add mixture to soup pot. Pour in reserved broth and chicken. Once heated, salt and pepper to taste. Cover and simmer for at least one hour. (It's best if cooked for several hours over very low heat. You may need the cans of broth if you plan to cook it more than an hour or need to stretch the amount of servings. You can also cook it the day before and just heat it up and serve in small bowls over cooked rice.)

*"Dinner" to a true Louisiana native is the meal in the middle of the day. Lunch is a relatively new word in the South. It began showing up in our vocabulary sometime in the 1970s. Supper is always served at night.

**The only trick to making a roux is not to burn it. You have to stir it constantly until it browns. Some people like it a pale brown, whereas others like a darker color brown. Try it each way, and see which you prefer. And if you have trouble getting your roux just right, e-mail or call a friend in Louisiana for advice!

Freda's Crawfish Bisque

The following is a great recipe from my friend Freda, who cohosts a fun party each Christmas. For a buffet, this bisque can be served in punch cups—spoons not needed.

1 pound peeled crawfish tails
½ bunch green onions, coarsely chopped
½ cup butter
½ cup onion, grated
2-3 garlic cloves, minced
½ cup flour
2 cups chicken stock, heated
2 cups half-and-half
2 cups heavy cream
1 teaspoon red pepper (or less)
2 teaspoons onion powder

Process the crawfish tails and green onions in a food processor until ground. Melt butter in large heavy saucepan and sauté the onion and garlic for 5 minutes. Add the flour and mix well. Cook for 2 minutes or until thickened, stirring constantly. Stir in the hot chicken stock and whisk. Simmer for 5 minutes, stirring constantly. Stir in the crawfish mixture. Simmer for 5 minutes, stirring frequently. Add the half-and-half and heavy cream and mix well. Simmer for 5 minutes, stirring occasionally. Stir in the red pepper and onion powder.

Partial to Pralines

Pralines are a favorite candy in Louisiana. As Christmas draws near, a woman in our community even sells them on the side of the road. For many years, I resisted trying to make pralines because I was afraid they'd be runny or too hard. My friend Sarah gave me this great praline recipe, and it's easy enough that I've even successfully made it! These make a good gift in a pretty tin or are a nice contribution to a party.

Sarah's Easy Pralines

1 large package vanilla pudding mix (not instant)
1 cup sugar
½ cup brown sugar
½ cup evaporated milk (not condensed)
1 tsp margarine
1 cup chopped pecans

Combine pudding, sugars, and milk in boiler. (Double boiler can be used but isn't necessary.) Cook over medium heat, stirring until sugar dissolves. Cook until mixture reaches full boil and then boil for 2 to 3 minutes (until good soft ball stage*). Remove from heat. Add margarine and nuts. Beat candy until it thickens. Drop by spoonsful onto waxed paper. Let set until firm.

A tip from Sarah: "The key to making these pralines is knowing when to start spooning them onto waxed paper. They harden pretty fast. Don't beat too long. (It's easy to beat them too long thinking they won't harden.)"

*Soft ball stage is when the mixture forms a soft ball when dropped in cold water. Keep a little dish of cold water by the stove and test the mixture every few minutes (getting fresh water each time). The longer it cooks, the firmer it will be in cold water. A variety of factors can affect how quickly pralines harden, but don't be afraid to give this recipe a try. The pralines are delicious, and people love them!

Freda's Chocolate Candy Shapes
Here's another candy recipe that is great for a party or gift.

2 cubes chocolate almond bark
2 tablespoons semisweet chocolate chips
2 tablespoons milk chocolate chips

Place all ingredients in microwave-safe bowl and microwave on high until melted, about 30 seconds; spoon chocolate mixture into candy molds. Put molds into freezer for 3-5 minutes or until firm; then pop candy out of molds. To keep, layer candy with waxed paper in candy tin. Candy has no preservatives and is best fresh.

Variations: Use all semisweet chocolate chips for dark chocolate candy. Use white almond bark and white chocolate chips for white chocolate candy. For color and a different flavor, crush peppermint sticks and add to candy molds before spooning chocolate into molds. Candy molds can be found at most arts and crafts stores.

Getting Together with Friends & Family

Gathering with friends and family can be one of the most fun parts of this season—and one of the most stressful. Sometimes we don't enjoy parties and holiday meals because we're so stressed trying to make everything perfect. Or, we want to have friends or relatives over but don't quite know how to fit it into our busy schedules.

People don't care how clean your house is or how fancy your food. They're happy to be invited for laughter, visiting, and enjoying a festive occasion. For many years, I've had the blessing to be invited to a party hosted by four dear friends. The two couples share responsibilities and planning for the occasion, and the party is a Christmas tradition we look forward to.

Why have a party? "Along with our two best friends, we wanted a special way to celebrate the Christmas season. Because of our combined love of music and food (one pianist, one soloist, two cooks), our annual Christmas Caroling Party began with twenty friends. Nearly twenty years later, we invite more than one hundred friends to celebrate with us. Over the years the food and friends have increased, but the true spirit of the season is always glorified by our singing carols and hymns around the piano."

How about you? Do you want to consider inviting friends or family (or both) over? What tradition might enrich your life and help others celebrate Christmas? Consider the following tips, with thanks to Freda for helping me compile them.

A Dozen Ways to Have a Happy Christmas Party

1. Make party choices that suit your style. Decide if you want fancy or casual, big crowd or handful of folks, lots of food or desserts only.

2. Let the occasion reflect your love and affection for those you invite.

3. Plan ahead, organize, plan ahead, organize, plan ahead! You and your guests will have a more enjoyable experience if you do.

4. Decide how big you want your party to be and what kind of food you'll serve. Do you want appetizers or desserts or a buffet meal? You could host a potluck and provide the main course then ask others to bring the rest. Remember: Do what fits you, an event you look forward to and enjoy hosting.

5. Consider asking friends to cohost.

6. Choose a date early and try to avoid overlap with community and church parties. Consider a "save the date" card or e-mail to help busy people plan. Don't give up because you can't find a date that suits everyone.

7. Send invitations by snail (postal) mail or e-mail.

8. Make a list of all the tasks you need help with on the day of the event and consider asking friends to help. Or, if the budget allows, hire someone. You might, for example, find students in a church youth group who would like to help as a fund-raiser. Consider: Who will be in charge of refilling dishes on a buffet? Who will take coats? Who will pick up empty plates and glasses?

9. Share chores to allow more time to visit and make guests feel welcome. Friends and family members are often delighted to help.

10. Make a schedule for the event itself—what time guests will arrive and what time you want to serve food. (Put appetizers out early.) Also, decide if you're going to sing carols, play a game, or do another activity; allow time for such things as preparing coffee and desserts or clearing the table.

11. Don't fret about little things. Spills happen, food gets cold, hungry guests arrive late, and so forth. Enjoy being together.

12. Ten to fifteen minutes before guests arrive, put your feet up and look forward to a fun party. Give thanks for those you love and the opportunity to gather.

A Picture-Perfect Touch

If you have friends or family over for Thanksgiving or Christmas, consider taking their photo as they arrive. You can mail them to guests as a memento or hand them out as they leave, if you have a printer.

For one party, my husband and I used an old Polaroid camera to photograph guests. We posted the pictures near the front door for enjoyment during the party. As guests left, we gave them their snapshots.

If you have a photo printer, you can ask someone to help print the pictures and give them to guests as they leave. You might ask older children to punch a hole in the top of pictures and attach ribbons for instant and personal ornaments.

Photographs of family and friends become special treasures as the years pass. Don't forget to snap a lot of pictures. Even the ones that don't seem "perfect" at the moment will grow in meaning as the years pass.

A Few Suggestions for Memorable Photos

1. Zoom in close and get facial expressions.
2. Be ready for the surprised look on the face, such as when a gift is opened.
3. Using a flash will freeze action but can also cause the dreaded red eye. Open curtains and turn on lights, and don't use the flash unless you have to.
4. Enjoy casual family shots, even taking pictures of children in PJs.
5. Plan ahead to get a good photo to include if you send Christmas cards. With the use of digital photography, you can take lots of different shots and weed out the ones you don't like.

—From Route 2 Photos (www.route2photos.com)

A Tried-and-True Tip When You're Feeling Overwhelmed: Grab a Quiet Moment

Despite our best efforts, some days we wind up feeling tired and cranky. When you find yourself rushing, allow yourself a few moments of quiet. Take a deep breath. If possible, sit down and put your feet up. Without taking much time at all, you can begin to feel renewed.

Consider this quiet time a gift to yourself. You'll find it gives you energy and enthusiasm for the many items on your to-do list!

You Can Make Quiet Moments Happen, No Matter How Busy You Are

1. Add quiet time to your schedule. It doesn't have to be long, but try to make it a habit. On the days you are busiest, you very likely need these quiet moments the most.

2. Consider ways to make your lunchtime less noisy and frenzied. Many people run errands and wind up feeling rushed. Allow a few quiet moments to refresh during your break.

3. Grab a few quiet moments between meetings or chores. Take a deep breath and line up your thoughts.

4. Give yourself permission to sit without feeling like you should be doing something else. Most of us are pretty good when it comes to *doing* things but not as good at simply *being*.

5. Use time in your car to recharge quietly. Allow a few extra minutes to get where you're going. The very act of moving slowly can help the din around you seem less annoying. While you're at it, turn off your phone and radio.

6. Pray or meditate. Remember your blessings.

7. Take a quiet stroll.

Enjoy Christmas Music

One of my favorite ways to relax at Christmas is to listen to music. I try to listen to favorite Christmas CDs every morning from Thanksgiving until Christmas Day. One collection of songs

often plays in my office during this season: *December*, piano solos
by George Winston (released by Windham Hill Records).
*I'd love to hear your favorite selections for Christmas. You can send
me a message to judy@judychristie.com.*

At-a-Glance Ways to Create a Christmas That Works For You

Shaping the Christmas you long for boils down to choices—your
choices, not those of a family member or friend or coworker.

Avoid Cookie-Cutter Christmases That Don't Work for You

1. Don't load yourself down with activities that drain you. If you
   find yourself feeling swamped, take something off your schedule.
2. Keep what's most important in mind. Spend energy on your
   priorities instead of activities that are not important or meaningful to you.
3. Don't do something just because everyone else is doing it. Do
   what works best for you.
4. Change your mind—and plans—when needed. Your daily
   decisions make your life busy or calm, peaceful or harried.

A Note on Awesome Advent Altars for Your Church

Mary Dark, who generously offered her family gumbo recipe,
also teaches people how to design creative and meaningful church

altars, including for Advent. Mary and I coauthored *Awesome Altars: How to Transform Worship Space* (Abingdon Press), and Mary leads workshops and provides how-to ideas on church altars. For more on Mary and how to use church altars to reflect the Christmas story, take a look at www.altarworks.com.

Advent Study of Hurry Less Worry Less at Christmas

Guide for Individual or Group Study

Readers across the country have asked for an Advent study guide for *Hurry Less, Worry Less at Christmas*, and it's my joy to provide four lessons here with

- Joyful Advent moments;
- A Bible passage related to the lesson;
- An Advent Idea to consider as you prepare your heart and life for Christmas and the New Year;
- Questions to apply to your life;
- A step to take in the week ahead.

The lessons can help you focus on the deep, spiritual core of Christmas and help you make everyday changes, eliminating the rush that too often steals Christmas peace.

Perhaps you want to do an individual study to step back from the hustle and bustle. Or maybe you have a group to bring together for Advent. You might also consider leading or participating in a churchwide Advent series, an approach that many churches take.

Hurry Less, Worry Less at Christmas can be used as a four-week study. Each session can last from one hour to an hour and a half, depending on the amount of time you allow for discussion.

Because participants are likely quite busy during this season, you want to be respectful of schedules and not let meetings last too long. Encourage participants to read chapters in advance and to ponder what God is doing in their lives.

A Sample Session

- Open with prayer and casual conversation and provide time for chatting as participants settle in.
- Direct participants to "Joyful Advent Moments" below, using this as an outline for the class.
- As the meeting begins, focus on the main Scripture for each chapter.
- Begin the lesson with "An Advent Idea."
- Lead the group in reading and discussing the "Questions to Consider."
- Ask group members to choose a step they will take during the coming week.
- Mention the chapters that will be discussed at the next meeting.
- Invite prayer requests as the lesson ends. Pray for God's guidance as each class member seeks to follow God's will and savor this special time of year. Give thanks for the birth of Jesus Christ.

Week One of Advent:
Creating a Hopeful Season Starting Right Now!
(Introduction and Chapters 1–3 of
Hurry Less, Worry Less at Christmas)

Joyful Advent Moments: Picture a joyful Christmas season. What does your ideal season from now until the New Year look like? Describe it.

Reflect on the Scripture: "Look! I bring good news to you— wonderful, joyous new for all people. Your savior is born today in David's city. He is Christ the Lord." (Luke 2:10-11 CEB)

An Advent Idea: Advent is a season of good news, a time for hope. Through small steps and daily decisions, we can change the busy world around us and help show that hope to others. Imagine that through our small, individual heartfelt efforts we might show our families and friends and coworkers and church members a new and better approach to Christmas.

Week One Questions to Consider
1. What does the good news of Christmas mean to you? What are you thankful for today? What brings you hope in your life?
2. Why do you think the world gets so busy during this time of year? What small changes might you make to simplify your Christmas season?
3. What is your favorite part of this season? What is your least favorite part? How can you do more of what you enjoy and trim some of what you don't like?

In the Week Ahead: Decide each morning to enjoy the day. Remember what Advent is about: giving thanks, the birth of Christ, our families, our friends.

Week Two of Advent: For God So Loved the World
(Chapters 4–5 of *Hurry Less, Worry Less at Christmas*)

Joyful Advent Moments: Advent is a time of anticipating the birth of Jesus and remembering how much God loves us. In what ways do you feel God's love in your life?

Reflect on the Scripture: *"Mary said,*
'With all my heart I glorify the Lord!
  In the depths of who I am I rejoice in God my savior.'"
(*Luke 1:46-47 CEB*)

An Advent Idea: This season, as our to-do lists get too long and our patience too short, we can choose instead to rejoice. Instead of getting grouchy and grinchy, we can glorify God. We can step back to take a fresh look at the many ways God blesses us every single day. We can encourage others, those who are alone or overwhelmed or just need a listening ear.

Week Two Questions to Consider
1. How might you glorify God in your everyday life? In what ways might you anticipate rather than dread the busy days ahead?

2. The word *love* is chosen to characterize the second week of Advent. How does that word reflect what Christmas is about? Who needs your love in a special way this season? Who might you encourage?

3. Many people overdo and overspend during "the Holidays." List activities you would like to do less of during this next week.

In the Week Ahead: Say thanks to God as you get up each day and be aware of the people you encounter each day, considering how you might show them the love of God.

Week Three of Advent: Tidings of Great Joy!
(Chapters 6–7 of *Hurry Less, Worry Less at Christmas*)

Joyful Advent Moments: Our joy is sometimes eroded by clinging to past traditions or trying to do too much. In what ways do you most need the great joy of Christmas?

Reflect on the Scripture: " 'Change your hearts and lives! Here comes the kindgom of heaven!' . . .
'Prepare the way for the Lord;
make his paths straight.' "
(Matthew 3:2-3 CEB)

An Advent Idea: This time of year can be joyful and exuberant, but it may also bring heartache. God's promises can ease our sorrow and guide us as we move forward. We can anticipate great things ahead—and know that God is with us if things do not go as we had hoped.

Week Three Questions to Consider
1. Christmas sometimes brings a mix of emotions. In what ways have you experienced that in your life? Do you see it in the lives of those around you?
2. In what ways might you need to change your heart and life in the midst of Advent?
3. What are you taking too seriously right now? In what ways are you trying to be perfect?

In the Week Ahead: Let go of something that you are holding onto too tightly. Do something just for fun!

Week Four of Advent: Peace on Earth . . . and in Your Heart
(Chapter 8 of *Hurry Less, Worry Less at Christmas*)

Joyful Advent Moments: God's peace can transcend our daily concerns. What worries or fears do you want to trust God to handle?

Reflect on the Scripture: "Peace I leave with you. My peace I give you. I give to you not as the world gives. Don't be troubled or afraid." (John 14:27 CEB)

An Advent Idea: Christmas Eve and Christmas Day bring a mixture of emotions and activities, but we need to focus on the message of that announcement: a Savior for all. Christ will bring peace to our lives in ways that we cannot begin to imagine.

Week Four Questions to Consider

1. Christ is called by many names: Immanuel, Messiah, Comforter, God with us. Which of those speaks to you most closely? What does "God with us" mean to you?
2. As you look back on Advent, what have you learned? What do you want to offer to God in the year ahead?
3. What will you focus on from now until the end of the year? What word might describe what you seek?

In the Week Ahead: Be flexible. Don't let bumps in the road or changes in plans dampen your holiday cheer. Remind yourself that God offers peace to you in your busy days.

Bonus Study: The New Year Ahead and Epiphany

The holiness of the Christmas season does not end on December 26. We can use the days that follow to prepare for a meaningful year ahead. A new year offers a great opportunity to take a fresh look at how we want to live. Epiphany, January 6, is a day that commemorates the birth of Jesus, the visit of the Magi, and Jesus' baptism and can be a time for spiritual growth.

New Year's and Epiphany
Living Abundantly in the Months Ahead
(Chapters 9–10 of *Hurry Less, Worry Less at Christmas*)

Joyful New Year Moments: God is on our daily journey with us and wants us to live abundantly, fully. How might you seek and use God's guidance in the days ahead?

Reflect on the Scripture: "Glory to God, who is able to do far beyond all that we could ask or imagine by his power at work within us; glory to him in the church and in Christ Jesus for all generations, forever and always. Amen." (Ephesians 3:20-21 CEB)

A New Year Idea: Epiphany and the start of the calendar year provide a time to look inward and reflect upon what Christ means in our lives. In the new year, we can grow into more of who God wants us to be. Let us commit to listening for and following God's direction.

Questions to Consider
1. What one or two areas of your life do you need to focus on most in the year ahead? home and family? work? spiritual life? finances? fitness? fun? What's most important to you? Why? How do your daily decisions reflect that priority?
2. People have many different feelings about goals. Have you ever set goals? How do you feel about goals? Why? Do you have ideas for how you want the new year to look? What small steps might you take to move forward in your life?

3. The wise men brought precious gifts to Jesus. What might you offer to God in the new year? Might you give more of your time to help others? spend additional time in prayer? become more involved in a community of faith? something else?

In the Week Ahead: Pray about what God wants you to do in your life this coming year and identify one thing you believe you need to do differently.

Thank you for sharing your Christmas journey with me.
May you be blessed with joyful moments, moments in which you are delighted and bring happiness to others, moments in which you give thanks, moments in which you lean into God's love and are renewed!
Rejoice during this special season!
—Judy Christie
www.judychristie.com